MEETING GOD

MEETING GOD

Carmelite Reflections
and Prayers

Irish Province of Carmelites

the columba press

First published in 2007 by
the columba press
55a Spruce Avenue, Stillorgan Industrial Estate,
Blackrock, Co Dublin

Design by Bill Bolger
Cover picture: Window of Our Lady of Mount Carmel,
Gort Muire, Ballinteer, Dublin. *Harry Clarke Studios*
Origination by The Columba Press
Printed in Ireland by ColourBooks, Ltd, Dublin

ISBN 978-1-85607-587-9

CONTENTS

St Albert of Jerusalem giving the Rule. Window by Frances Biggs in Terenure College Chapel, Dublin.

INTRODUCTION

This book of Carmelite reflections and prayers presents
some samples from the rich heritage with which God has
blessed Carmel over a period of eight centuries.

The Carmelite Order takes its origin from Mount
Carmel where hermits began to gather towards the end of
the 12th century. They approached St Albert, Patriarch of
Jerusalem, for a 'way of life' sometime after 1206. This
letter was approved by Pope Innocent III in 1247 and
became known as the *Rule of St Albert*. To mark St Albert's
letter to the hermits, the Irish Province of Carmelites
(O. Carm.) wished to share with its friends and the wider
Church something of the riches of its tradition.

The variety offered by this book is itself an invitation
to use it in many ways. It is certainly not meant to be
read through. It is a book to be used at various times to
find prayers and inspiration. It needs time to disclose the
riches of its many short passages. It is to be taken up and
pondered. It can become a friend at the bedside or in the
kitchen or the office, a book for the bus or car. The lives
and writings of Carmelite saints and spiritual writers are
meant to be a word for our time, for our overbusy and
secularised world.

May those who use this little book experience the
blessing of Our Lady of Mount Carmel and of the saints
of Carmel.

The medieval Carmelite crest has twelve stars representing Our Lady, the sword of Elijah, his words which are the Carmelite motto, 'With zeal I have been zealous for the Lord God of hosts' (1 Kings 19:14).

The high point between the two central stars symbolises Mount Carmel. The meaning of the Carmelite three stars is disputed: an early explanation is that they represent three patrons of the Order: Mary, Elijah and Albert of Trapani.

CARMELITE PATRONS

Our Lady of Mount Carmel
and the Prophet Elijah

Shrine of Our Lady of Dublin. Carved oak statue from School of Dürer (c. 15th century) in Whitefriar Street Church.

OUR LADY OF MOUNT CARMEL

The Carmelite Order has always been regarded as Marian by the People of God. In addition to devotion to Our Lady of Mount Carmel throughout the Church, there is also apparent reinforcement in apparitions which allude to the title or image of Our Lady of Mount Carmel, or which have significant appearances on 16 July.

Early history

At the beginning times of the Order, the *Rule* specified that there be an oratory in the middle of the hermit cells; the Carmelites chose to dedicate this church to St Mary. She thus becomes the Lady of the Place. In medieval culture this amounts to the choice of Mary as Patron: Carmelites will serve her; she will look after them.

When the Carmelites came to Europe they found there already a rich culture of devotion to Mary. Quite soon Carmelites were called 'Brothers of the Blessed Virgin Mary of Mount Carmel.' By the end of the 14th century the Carmelite family looked to two inspirational figures, Mary and Elijah; they were its foundational figures in the sense that all the Order sought was seen to be already incarnated in the lives of the Prophet and the Mother.

11

Devotion

Devotion grows by reflection, prayer and study. It may be strengthened not only by saying prayers or invoking Mary's intercession, but also by doing things in her honour. Medieval devotion emphasised simple gestures like bowing at the mention of Mary's name, as well as processions, candles, etc. Carmelite art, like the *La Bruna* (The Brown Lady) image in Naples, shows a special tenderness in the depiction of Mary and her Son. A true Carmelite vision will never separate Mary from Jesus.

The highest devotion celebrates Mary in the liturgy. We have not only the Masses of Our Lady of Mount Carmel with their rich texts and splendid prefaces, but also many feasts of Mary in the universal Church which the Carmelite Family should celebrate with particular joy.

Mary and Carmel

When we survey the rich Marian tradition of Carmel, we might summarise it by saying that Mary is a gentle presence, always there with the Carmelite. Sometimes we feel her presence as Mother, at other times as Sister, Patroness or Model. One of the most common titles given to Mary in the Order is Mother and Beauty of Carmel. A vision of her beauty can always be refreshment for us in the harshness of secular society.

There are five truths about Mary in the Carmelite Order, not all equally emphasised in any particular century.

They are not exclusive to the Order, but they show its preferences in reflecting on the Mother of God:

Mary is *Mother*. Carmelites took up this Church teaching with great enthusiasm. But they added another word, so that 'Mother and Beauty of Carmel' became a preferred name for her.

Secondly, Mary is also seen as *Patron* of Carmelites. This is a medieval concept that implies a two-way relationship between lord and servant: the lord protected his servants; they in turn looked after his interests. Such a concept fitted admirably the Carmelite vision of Mary as one whom they loved and served, and who in turn protected them.

Again, Mary is also *Sister* of Carmelites. The idea of Mary as Sister is found also in the first millennium, and in the papal teaching of Paul VI. When we speak of Mary as Sister, we are reminded that she too is one like us, is a daughter of Adam, and that she had to walk the same path of faith, hope and love as all people. The Carmelite idea of Mary as Sister can also have something of the idea of an elder, caring sister who looks after the rest of the family. We can look up to our Sister and accept her guidance. At different times we may be more drawn to the idea of Mary as Sister, rather than as Mother. Both are legitimate, but we should not deny the validity of a title that may not attract us at a particular time.

Fourthly, Mary is the *Most Pure Virgin*. This title, very common in Carmelite saints and writers, looks especially to Mary's purity of heart. She retained God's word in her heart (see Luke 2:19, 51) and she served him with an undivided and pure heart.

Mary is a *Model* for Carmelites. We can look at what she did. But we have to go deeper. It is not just a matter of doing what Mary did, but having her attitude in all our thoughts and actions.

The Brown Scapular

Medieval devotion to Our Lady of Mount Carmel spread outside the friars, nuns and Third Order members, especially through the scapular. It was a reduced form of the Carmelite habit. It was a sign of affiliation to the Order, often made more public through the Archconfraternity of Our Lady of Mount Carmel. The details of its origins are far less significant than its approval by the Church over many centuries. A recent document of the Holy See on popular devotions (2002) has strongly commended the scapular. It noted that its use is very defuse and often independent of the life and spirituality of the Order. The Vatican document also notes: 'It is an external sign of the filial relationship established between the Blessed Virgin Mary, Mother and Queen of Carmel, and the faithful who entrust themselves totally to her protection, who have recourse to her maternal intercession, who are mindful of the primacy of the spiritual life and the need for prayer.' (n. 205)

Carmelite saints

All the saints of Carmel in their own ways are characterised by devotion to Mary. Carmelite mystics like St Teresa of Avila have enjoyed visions or locutions, that is, words from Mary. St Thérèse of Lisieux had a deep familiar relationship with the one whom she described as 'more Mother than Queen'. Bl Isidore Bakanja was a farm labourer in Belgian Congo (Zaïre). An atheist employer flogged him for wearing a scapular and a rosary around his neck. He died from his wounds in 1909. Coming from a Jewish culture and being an early feminist, St Teresa Benedicta of the Cross (Edith Stein) gives us rich insights into Mary as mother and as woman.

Presence

A renewed devotion to Mary is not primarily a matter of saying more prayers to her. It implies a relationship with her, which will be established by prayer and reflected in imitation. There is a huge difference between knowing about a person, and really knowing them. Renewal in our Marian life is not a matter of prayers or information, but a loving knowing.

Such a knowing loving, or loving knowing, lies behind the idea of presence. We know that we are always in the presence of God, who sustains us, keeps us in being. But we may not be alert to this presence as we go about our daily lives. It is good to stop occasionally and reflect that we are always in God's presence.

The gentle presence of Mary is found in her caring for all the Church, in her continuous prayer for us, 'now and at the hour of our death' (*Hail Mary*). We can become aware of her presence if we think of her now and again, speak to her, ask for her guidance, and consider how she would act in the circumstances in which we may find ourselves. We can go further and enjoy and relax in her presence.

Every age in the Church finds new insights into God's plan unfolded in the Mother of the Son of God. The Carmelite Order also continues its own exploration of its Marian heritage.

MEDIEVAL PRAYERS

Grant to your servants we beseech thee O Lord, unfailing health of mind and body, and through the intercession of the glorious and blessed ever Virgin Mary may we be saved from present sorrow and enjoy future joy.

– Carmelite Constitutions (1281)

Protect, O Lord, your servants with the support of peace; as they are confident of the patronage of the Blessed Virgin Mary, keep them safe from all enemies.

– Carmelite Constitutions (1324)

Elijah from Rose Window in White Abbey, Kildare.

THE PROPHET ELIJAH

In the Basilica of St Peter's Rome, there is a statue of the prophet Elijah with the inscription: 'The entire Carmelite Order erected this statue to its founder.' The statue faces Sts Dominic, Benedict, and Francis of Assisi. There was controversy before and after the erection of the fine statue by Cornacchini in 1727: many denied the truth of the claim of Carmelites that Elijah was their founder, in the sense of the other thirty-seven founding figures in St Peter's.

Today Carmelites would not see their Order going back in an historical line to the prophet who flourished more than 800 years before Christ. But there are spiritual links. The first Carmelites venerated the prophet, and established themselves near the fountain called Elijah's on Mount Carmel. Moreover they saw their life as in spiritual succession to that of the prophet.

Elijah was one of the greatest of the prophets; he appeared with Moses at the Transfiguration (Lk 9:28-36); many people at the time thought that John the Baptist and also Jesus might have been Elijah returning as promised in the Old Testament (Mal 4:5-6; see Sir 48:1-11).

The history of Elijah is found in 1 Kings 17 to 2 Kings 2. There we find a multifaceted figure that has attracted the contemplation of Carmelites over the centuries. There are dramatic moments as when he proclaimed a drought in Israel and conquered the prophets of Baal (1 Kgs 17-18); he was a loyal prophet speaking the word of God. He successfully outwitted the evil King Ahab and his wicked wife Jezebel. He was a protector of the poor, for example the widow of Zaraphat (1 Kgs 17:8-24); he condemned the murder of Naboth planned by the queen and he proclaimed God's judgement against them (1 Kgs 21).

But Elijah was also frail and lapsed into discouragement and self-pity, until restored by God in the vision upon Mount Horeb (Sinai). He was strengthened by an angel who fed him so that he could walk to the holy mountain. When he arrived there he complained to God that he had been forsaken, even though he could say, 'I have been zealous for the Lord God of hosts' (1 Kgs 19:10 – these words later became the motto of the Carmelite Order). God surprised Elijah not by an appearance in a great wind, earthquake or fire, but in the sound of sheer silence (1 Kgs 19:11-14). He resumed his prophetic ministry and some time later he was taken up into heaven in a fiery chariot, leaving behind his disciple Elisha to continue on as prophet.

At different times in its history the Carmelite Order has looked to one or more aspects of the prophet's life: he is active and contemplative; one who heard and spoke the word of God; a friend of the dispossessed. The Carmelite Constitutions in 1995 give a fine summary of what Elijah means to the Order today:

In Elijah we see the solitary prophet who nurtured his thirst for the one and only God, and lived in his presence. He is the contemplative, burning with passionate love for the Absolute who is God, 'his word flaring like a torch' (Sir 48:1). He is the mystic, who after a long and wearisome journey, learned to read the new signs of God's presence. He is the prophet who became involved in the lives of the people, and who, by battling against false idols, brought them back to faithfulness to the Covenant with the One God. He is the prophet who was in solidarity with the poor and the forgotten, and who defended those who endured violence and injustice. From Elijah, Carmelites learn to be people of the desert, with heart undivided, standing before God and entirely dedicated to his service, uncompromising in the choice to serve God's cause, aflame with a passionate love for God. Like Elijah, they believe in God and allow themselves to be led by the Spirit and by the Word that has taken root in their hearts, in order to bear witness to the divine presence in the world, allowing God to be truly God in their lives. Finally, in Elijah they learn to be channels of God's tender love for the poor and humble.

– Constitutions (1995) 26

Blessed Titus Brandsma Window by Frances Biggs in Terenure College, Chapel, Dublin.

CARMELITE WITNESS
THROUGH THE CENTURIES

ST PETER THOMAS

(CA. 1305-1366)

Feast 8 January

The life of Peter Thomas (Thomas is perhaps a surname) is complex and fascinating, marked by extraordinary achievement. Born into a very poor family in southern Périgord, France about 1305, he left home and sought education, supporting himself by teaching others. In his life he always felt the help of the Virgin Mary. He entered the Carmelites at the age of twenty-one. He continued study, taught theology, and as procurator general of the Order at Avignon he became noticed by several popes. He was appointed papal legate and diplomat on many missions, spending his energies mainly on seeking reunion with Christians separated from Rome. He was named Archbishop of Crete in 1363 and Patriarch of Constantinople a year later. He died at Famagusta in Cyprus in 1366. Though it may stretch a point to call him an early ecumenist (his approach and methods were not today's), he still testifies to the importance and urgency of work for Christian unity and peace.

Lord you inspired in your bishop St Peter Thomas an intense desire to promote peace and Christian unity. Following his example may we live steadfast in the faith and work perseveringly for peace. Through Christ our Lord. Amen.

– From the Carmelite liturgy

'To sing to your name Lord, is my joy, the delight of my heart.'

'The Lord will honour the gentle and deliver them.'

'Relying on the power of God, I bear hardships for the sake of the gospel, for I have been appointed its herald and teacher.'

'Today on his feast he returned home, a glorious son of the Church and a tiller in the field of faith; today he entered God's mystery, this preacher of the Cross and of the truth; today this soldier of the faith, strong in word and deed, is filled with eternal mercy.'

– Antiphons from Carmelite liturgy for his feast

Blessed Nuno Alvares Window in Whitefriar Street Church, Dublin.

BL NUNO ALVARES PEREIRA

(1360-1431)

Feast, April 1

Even as an aristocrat and military leader, who was to the fore in the fight for the independence of Portugal, Nuno Alvares Pereira was a very devout man, especially attached to the Eucharist, to the Virgin Mary and noted for his charitable works. Some thirty-eight years after the death of his wife and by then a national hero, Nuno entered the Carmelite Order as a lay brother in 1423. The remaining eight years of his life were marked by penance, prayer and quite remarkable humility.

Mary Mother of Carmel, I reverence your holy Scapular and thank you for this gift. Guide and help me always as I place my confidence in your intercession. Never was it known, dear Mother, that anyone who fled to your intercession was left unaided.

– Prayer of Bl Nuno

Lord God, you called Blessed Nuno Alvares Pereira to put aside his sword and follow Christ under the patronage of Our Lady of Mount Carmel. Through his prayers may we too deny ourselves and be devoted to you with all our hearts. Through Christ our Lord. Amen.

– Prayer from Carmelite liturgy

ST GEORGE PRECA

(1888-1942)

Feast 9 May

George Preca was born in Valletta, Malta on 12 February 1880. He was ordained a diocesan priest in 1906. He had some premonitions that he should be committed to evangelisation. His deceased confessor, Fr Aloysius Galea, appeared to him a few days after his death saying: 'God has chosen you to teach his people.' He brought a group of laymen together for the purpose, called the Society of Christian Doctrine (with a Maltese acronym MUSEUM), but Church authorities were afraid of what they saw as inadequately educated lay people teaching the faith. George's movement was banned for a while. He was thus an early promoter of lay ministry.

Fr Preca trusted in the maternal protection of Our Lady. He became a member of the Carmelite Third Order and at his profession in September 1919 chose the name of Fr Franco. In 1957 he suggested the use of five 'Mysteries of Light' for the private recitation of the Rosary, a proposal formally adopted by Pope John II in his encyclical on the Rosary (2004). George Preca was beatified in 2001 and canonised in 2007.

Around 1910 George had a very powerful mystical experience. He saw a twelve-year-old boy pushing a low cart with a bag full of manure. The boy turned to George and ordered him imperiously: 'Lend me a hand!' He later understood, however, that the boy was Jesus, and that the Lord was asking him and his followers to help him with nurturing the Lord's field and vineyard with sound doctrine and formation. One of George Preca's methods of prayer was to go in front of the Tabernacle and pray by reminding Christ of a story from his life. He named this prayer 'The exercise of Friar Franco' (his Carmelite name). His motto was: 'With Christ, in Christ and for Christ'.

Lord God, you granted countless favors to St George Preca, choosing him as a most faithful instrument in founding the Society of Christian Doctrine. Grant that I also learn to turn all circumstances and events of my life into opportunities to love you and serve the Church and all humanity, lighting up the corners of the world with faith hope and love. Through Christ our Lord. Amen.

– Prayer of his followers

ST SIMON STOCK
(D. CIRCA 1265)

Feast, 16 May

Simon, an Englishman, is traditionally remembered as an early prior general of the Order sometime after 1240. This was a time of great difficulty, as Carmelites sought to settle in Europe as friars having been forced by persecution to leave Mount Carmel. His memory is associated with the origin of the Brown Scapular, a devotion which later received the highest approval from Church authorities as a means of relating to the Blessed Virgin. Simon is recalled for his personal holiness and his devotion to the Blessed Virgin. There is extensive devotion to him in Bordeaux where he was buried. A relic was sent from Bordeaux to the restored friary at Aylesford in 1951. The *Flos Carmeli*, though of a later date, has been traditionally associated with Simon Stock. Its sentiments clearly reflect the attitude of 13th century Carmelites to Our Lady of Mount Carmel.

Flower of Carmel
Flos Carmeli,
Blossoming vine,
Vitis florigera,
Splendour of heaven,
Splendor Coeli,
Childbearing Virgin
Virgo puerpera
None equals thee.
Singularis.
Mother so tender,
Mater mitis
Whom no man dost know,
Sed viri nescia
On Carmel's children
Carmelitis
Thy favours bestow,
Esto propitia
Star of the sea
Stella maris

ST MARY MAGDALENE DE'PAZZI

(1556-1607)

Feast 25 May

The De'Pazzi was a noble Florentine family. Called after Catherine of Siena, she was born in that city in 1556. Her childhood was devout. At the age of sixteen she entered the Carmel in Florence; she chose that convent because of the practice of frequent Holy Communion there. She took the name of Mary Magdalene. In the convent for the first five years she experienced numerous temptations and trials. From the age of thirty-four she experienced many remarkable ecstasies and other graces. As she spoke during these and the sisters wrote them down, we have a rich source of spiritual teaching, especially on the Trinity and on the Passion of Jesus, in five volumes. The centre of her life was the liturgy and she has left us very significant prayers, especially to the Trinity and to the Holy Spirit. She was notable too for her devotion to Mary. In the last three years of her life the ecstasies largely ceased and she was left to combat serious ill health and spiritual darkness. She was canonised in 1669.

Come, Holy Spirit, may the union of the Father and the will of the Son come to us. You, Spirit of truth, are the reward of saints, the refreshment of souls, light in darkness, the riches of the poor, the treasury of lovers, the satisfaction of the hungry. Come, you who descending into Mary, caused the Word to take flesh; bring about in us by grace what you did in her by grace and nature. Come, you who are the nourishment of all chaste thoughts, the fountain of all clemency, the summit of all purity. Come and take away from us all that hinders us from being absorbed in you. Amen.

– Dialogues and Enlightenments 4

BL JOHN SORETH

(1394-1471)

Feast 24 July

John Soreth was born near Caen in Normandy. He
joined the Carmel in that town and was ordained about
1417. He studied in Paris becoming a university master of
theology. He was provincial in France from 1440 and
became prior general of the whole Order eleven years
later, remaining so until his death in 1471. He is best
remembered as committed to the reform of the Order, in
pursuit of which he travelled to most of the provinces.
He wrote a long commentary on the Carmelite *Rule* in
which he is particularly strong on the religious vows,
especially poverty. He was diplomatic in dealing with
reform movements that might have broken away from the
Order. He was also responsible for regularising the state
of various groups of women who wished to be members
of the Order especially after he obtained the bull, *Cum
nulla,* from the pope in 1452. This can be regarded as a
founding charter of both the second order of nuns and of
the third order of lay Carmel. He was beatified in 1866.
He is usually represented with a pyx in his hand, recalling
the occasion when with great risk to his life, he saved
consecrated Hosts from desecration during the devast-
ation of the city of Liège.

It is from Christ himself that you will learn how to love him. Learn to love him tenderly, with all your heart; prudently with all your soul; fervently with all your strength. Love him tenderly, so that you will not be seduced away from him; prudently, that you will not be open to deception; fervently so that downheartedness will not draw you away from Christ's love. May the wisdom of Christ seem delightful to you, so that you are not led away by the glory of the world or pleasures of the flesh. May Christ, who is the Truth, enlighten you, so that you do not fall prey to the spirit of error and falsehood. May Christ, who is the strength of God, fortify you when hardships wear you out. So let the love of Christ kindle your enthusiasm; let his knowledge be your teacher and his constancy be your strength.

– From Bl John Soreth's Commentary on the Rule

BL TITUS BRANDSMA

(1881-1942)

Feast 27 July

Anno Brandsma was born in Friesland (northern Netherlands) in 1881. He entered the Carmelite Order when seventeen, taking the name Titus. He did his novitiate in Boxmeer, a town traditionally famous for its Eucharistic devotion. He studied in Rome; eventually after some delay due to ill-health, he obtained a PhD at the Gregorian University in 1909. Poor health was to prove a life-long problem for him.

He became professor of philosophy and the history of mysticism in the new Catholic University in Nijmegen, becoming rector in 1932. All his life he was involved in writing, publishing and journalism. In 1935 he became spiritual director of the union of Dutch Catholic journalists. As such he encouraged opposition to Nazi propaganda and especially its anti-Semitism. He was arrested January 1942 and was in a series of prisons, ending up in Dachau where, after dreadful medical experimentation on him, he was killed by lethal injection, 26 July 1942. He was beatified in 1985.

O Jesus when I look at you,
My love for you again lights up,
And your heart moreover treasures me,
Even as a special friend of yours.

Courage and suffering are demanded,
But all suffering is good for me,
For through it I become like you,
Finding thus the Kingdom path.

I am truly fortunate in my pain,
Which I no longer sense as hurt,
For it's more a loving plan
That makes me one with you, O God.

Oh, leave me here alone and still,
With chill and cold surrounding me,
And let no person come to me,
For being alone doesn't weary me.

Remain then with me, Jesus
I was never so close to you,
Stay with me, Jesus, my delight,
Your presence here makes all things good.

– Written in Scheveningen prison 12-13 February 1942.
Translation: Gort Muire

ST ALBERT OF TRAPANI

(d. 1307)

Feast 7 August

Albert is variously called 'of Trapani' (from his birth-place), or 'degli Abati' (his family name). He was born in Sicily in the mid-thirteenth century. He is recalled in Carmelite history as an outstanding preacher and miracle-worker. He was among the first Carmelite saints venerated in the Order and was long considered its patron and protector.

Several general chapters and priors general stipulated that his image should to be placed in every Carmelite house. Various images show the following symbols: he is usually with a book or bible indicating his preaching, with a lily recalling the purity of his life and often in the act of overcoming the devil and, later still, working miracles. He is also represented with the child Jesus in his arms and sometimes driving away the devil with his foot. A popular devotion has been St Albert's Water, blessed with his relic and used against fever and other illness.

Lord God you made St Albert of Trapani a model of purity and prayer, and a devoted servant of Our Lady. May we practise these same virtues and so be worthy always to share in the banquet of your grace. Through Christ our Lord. Amen.

– Carmelite Liturgy

O my God, you have created the human race by your wonderful power. It is an act of your clemency that has called us to share your glory and eternal life. When the first sin condemned us to suffer death, out of your goodness you wished to redeem us through the blood of your Son, to unite us to you through our faith and your great mercy. You have bought us back from the shame of our sin; you have veiled our dishonour in the brightness of your glory. Look now and see that what you have created, giving it subtle limbs and joints and made beautiful through its immortal soul, is now subject to the attack of Satan. Be pleased Lord to reconstitute your work and heal it. May your power be glorified and may the malice of the enemy be stunned.

– Prayer for healing attributed to Saint Albert

ST TERESA BENEDICTA OF THE CROSS
— EDITH STEIN

(1891-1942)

Feast 9 August

Edith Stein was born into a Jewish family, her mother being particularly devout. She lost her Jewish faith in her teens and went to study philosophy under the renowned Edmund Husserl. Later she was attracted to the Church by the example of Catholics and other Christians, and by reading through in one night the autobiography of St Teresa of Avila. Apart from philosophical papers, as an academic she wrote extensively on matters of education, and on women's issues. Edith's teaching was curtailed by the Nazis and she entered Carmel in Cologne in 1933 taking the name Sr Teresa Benedicta of the Cross. With heightened persecution in Germany she transferred to the Carmel at Echt in Holland. She was arrested there and sent with her blood sister Rosa to Auschwitz where she was gassed in 1942. Leaving the convent she said to her sister, 'Come Rosa. We are going for our people.' Three years earlier she stated that she wished her death to be offered for the Carmelite Order especially in Cologne and Echt, for the Jewish people, for the salvation of Germany, for world peace and for all her relatives living and dead. Edith was canonised in 1998 and declared co-patron of Europe 1999.

We need to have traditional forms and to participate in public and prescribed services of worship, so that our interior life will remain vital and on the right track, and so will find appropriate expression … The way to the interior life is Christ. His blood is the curtain through which we enter the Holiest of Holies, the Divine Life. In baptism and in the sacrament of penance, his blood cleanses us of our sins, opens our eyes to eternal light, our ears to hearing God's word. It opens our lips to sing his praise, to pray in expiation, in petition, in thanksgiving, all of which are but varying forms of adoration, that is, the creature's homage to the Almighty and All benevolent One.

– Article 'On the prayer of the Church' (1936)

O my God, fill my soul with holy joy, courage and strength to serve you. Enkindle your love in me and then walk with me along the next stretch of road before me. I do not see very far ahead, but when I have arrived where the horizon now closes down, a new prospect will open before me and I shall meet with peace.

– Prayer of St Teresa Benedicta of the Cross

BL MARY OF JESUS CRUCIFIED
(1846-1878)

Feast 25 August

Called 'The Little Arab' by a biographer, Mariam Baouardy was born in Galilee but was orphaned at the age of three and was brought up by an uncle in Alexandria. At a time of religious ferment, a Moslem, who wanted her to convert to Islam, wounded her seriously. Left for dead, she believed herself cured by the Blessed Virgin. She avoided an arranged marriage and entered into domestic service at Beirut, Jerusalem and at Marseilles, where she tried her vocation in an active congregation. She received the stigmata when she was twenty-one. Because of extraordinary mystical experiences even as a novice, she was advised to join a contemplative order and she entered Carmel at Pau. She was soon sent to India where she was professed in 1871. Her mystical graces were misunderstood and consequentially she had to return to France. She planned a foundation of a Carmel near Bethlehem which was established in 1876. She was arranging for a foundation at Nazareth when she died in 1878. She had little education, but was a profound and acute spiritual guide. She was beatified in 1983.

I am in God, and God is in me. I feel that all creatures, all trees and flowers belong to God and to me. I have no will, it belongs to God; what is God's is mine. It is only love that can fill the human heart. A just person who has love and just a pinch of earth is fully satisfied; an evil person filled with pleasures, honours and riches is always hungry, always thirsty, and will never be satisfied. Pay attention to small things; everything is great before the Lord. He does not want plunder in sacrifices; give him all. In heaven the most beautiful trees are those who have most sinned; they have used their miseries like dung around their roots.

Holy Spirit, inspire me. Love of God, consume me. On the true path, lead me. Mary my Mother, look on me; with Jesus bless me. From every evil, from every illusion, from every danger, preserve me.

– Prayers during ecstasies

ST THÉRÈSE OF LISIEUX

(1873-1897)

Feast 1 October

Thérèse Martin was born at Alençon in Normandy, France in 1873. She lost her mother at an early age, but her home was warm and loving. After much opposition she entered the Carmel at Lisieux at the age of fifteen. She took the name Thérèse of the Child Jesus and of the Holy Face. Life was difficult for her there: she experienced much ill health and deep spiritual darkness for the final eighteen months of her life; she died at the age of twenty-four. She was canonised in 1925 and made co-patron of the missions two years later. She was proclaimed a doctor of the Church in 1997. Her spiritual doctrine stresses God's love and mercy to which she responded by spiritual childhood, an attitude of complete love and confidence in God. It is largely summarised in her phrase, 'the Little Way.' She saw her life as being 'love in the heart of the Church'. She is popularly called 'The Little Flower' because of her promise to send flowers, that is, divine favours, on the world after her death.

O God, I offer you all that I am going to do today, with and for the glory of the Sacred Heart of Jesus I want to conquer my faults by casting them into the furnace of his merciful love. O my God, I ask for myself and for those dear to me the grace of perfectly doing your will, of accepting for your love all the joys and pains of this passing life so that we may one day be united for eternity in heaven. Amen.

O Jesus, I would be happy if I had been very faithful. But in the evening I am often sad, since I could have responded better to your graces. If I had been more united to you, more loving with my sisters, more humble and more mortified, I would have less embarrassment when meeting you in prayer. However, my God, far from being discouraged at the sight of my misery, I come to you with every confidence, remembering that 'those who are healthy do not need the doctor, but the sick'. I ask you to heal me and to pardon me; for my part I will keep in mind that 'the one who has been forgiven much, should love you more than others'.

– *Prayers of St Thérèse*

ST TERESA OF JESUS [OF AVILA]
(1515-1582)

Feast 15 October

Teresa de Ahumada was born in Avila in 1515. She entered the Carmelite Order at the age of twenty. The early years, and indeed her whole life, were marked by poor health. The first eighteen years of her Carmelite life were not noticeable by any great fervour; she had a major conversion experience about 1556 after which she received many mystical graces. She felt called to live a more authentic life and she embarked on a reform movement that eventually gave rise to the Discalced Carmelites who became a separate branch of the Order after her death. St John of the Cross was a close companion of this reform. Her writings include three classics of Christian spirituality: *The Life; The Way of Perfection; The Interior Castle.* She was not only profoundly gifted in prayer, but also a teacher of prayer. She died in 1582, was canonised in 1622 and declared a doctor of the Church in 1970.

Let nothing trouble you,
Let nothing scare you
All is fleeting.
God alone is unchanging.
Patience obtains all.
Whoever possesses God,
Wants nothing,
God alone suffices.

Nada te turbe,
Nada te espante,
Todo se pasa,
Dios no se muda.
La paciencia
Toto lo alcanza;
Quien a Dios tiene
Nada le falta
Sólo Dios basta.

BL FRANCES D'AMBOISE
(1427-1485)

Feast 5 November

Frances was born of a noble family in Thouars, France. At the age of fifteen she married Peter II, Duke of Brittany. With much endurance she brought him around to deep piety so that his reign was a time of peace and Christian standards. He died seven years after ascending the ducal throne at Rennes in 1450. Frances had as a spiritual director, Blessed John Soreth. Under his guidance she became a Carmelite nun in 1468 and made other foundations in France. These were noted for very strict enclosure and for frequent Communion. She is acknowledged as the foundress of Carmelite nuns in France. Religious images often show her dressed in a Carmelite habit, with a cloak of ermine to designate her former state as duchess. She died in 1485 and her cult was approved by Pius IX in 1863.

Whatever the troubles and difficulties that weigh you down, bear them all patiently and keep in mind that these are the things which constitute your cross. There is always something to be endured, and if you refuse one cross, be sure that you will meet with another, maybe a heavier one. One who is never tried acquires little virtue. You have various afflictions which constitute your cross. Bear them willingly to the very end, and you will finally yield your soul to God. Give him praise and thanks for calling you into his service. When the Lord sees your good will and your perseverance, he will give you the support of his grace, enabling you to sustain to the end the burdens of religious life. Through his love nothing will be too difficult for you.

– From her Exhortations to her nuns

BL ELIZABETH OF THE TRINITY

(1880-1906)

Feast 8 November

Elizabeth Catez was born in 1880 in the diocese of Bourges, France. A very gifted pianist, she announced at the age of fourteen that she wished to enter Carmel. Her mother, then a widow, opposed this move and tried to dissuade her by all kinds of social activities. Elizabeth learned to live at two levels: an outer one that people could see; a deeper level as she reached down to the core of her being where Jesus dwelt. She entered the Carmel at Dijon in 1901 and died five years later; she was beatified in 1984.

The spiritual doctrine of Elizabeth is centred around presence: the presence of Jesus in her heart; the divine indwelling of the Trinity in her being. This latter she described as her 'heaven on earth'. Midway through her life in Carmel she discovered the text 'To the praise of his glory' (Eph 1:14), which unified everything in her life: her excruciating last illness, the darkness in which God led her and her Carmelite vocation at the service of the Church. Her prayer, 'Trinity whom I adore,' remains one of the treasures of Christian devotion. (See pp 137-8.)

A Carmelite, my darling, is a soul who has gazed on the Crucified, who has seen him offering himself to his Father as a Victim for souls and, recollecting herself in this great vision of the charity of Christ, has understood the passionate love of his soul and has wanted to give herself as he did! ... And on the mountain of Carmel, in silence, in solitude, in prayer that never ends, for it continues through everything, the Carmelite already lives as if in heaven: by God alone. The same One who will one day be her beatitude and will fully satisfy her in glory is already giving himself to her. He never leaves her, he dwells within her soul; more than that, the two of them are but one. So she hungers for silence that she may always listen, penetrate ever deeper into his Infinite Being. She is identified with him whom she loves, she finds him everywhere; she sees him shining through all things! Is not this heaven on earth! You carry this heaven within your soul, my little Germaine, you can be a Carmelite already.

– Letter n. 133 to her cousin Germaine de Gemeaux, 1902

ST JOHN OF THE CROSS

(1542-1591)

John was born at Fontiveros, Spain about 1542. His father, Gonzalo, married a poor weaver Catalina knowing that he would be disinherited and live in poverty as a result. John learned several trades as a youth and, having obtained some education with the Jesuits, entered the Carmelite Order at the age of twenty-one. After ordination he wished to have a more solitary life, but he was persuaded by Teresa of Avila to remain in Carmel and help with her reform. This decision led to much persecution and hardship right until his death in 1591. He was canonised in 1726 and declared a doctor of the Church in 1926.

A much admired poet of the Spanish language, for many people his poems are a way of entry into his writings. His major works describe and explain the spiritual journey from initial conversion to the highest states of mystical love. He sees profoundly into the spiritual sickness of our being, but only to show how loving God (as his father loved Catalina) and being open to divine love leads to transformation. He is famous for insisting on *nada* (nothing apart from God) and for his teaching on nights, which are times when we struggle to avoid sin and develop virtue, and times when God heals and purifies us in darkness.

The Virgin, weighed
With the Word of God
Comes down the road;
If only you'll shelter her.

– Poem 14

Forgetfulness of creation
Remembrance of the Creator
Attention to what is within
And to be loving the Beloved.

– Poem 15

'In tribulation, immediately draw near to God in fear and truth and you will receive strength, enlightenment and instruction.'

'At the evening of life, you will be examined in love. Learn how to love as God desires to be loved and abandon your own way of acting.'

'Those who grumble or complain, are not perfect, nor are they even good Christians.'

'The Father spoke one Word, which was his Son, and this Word he always speaks in eternal silence, and in silence must it be heard by the soul.'

– Sayings

BR LAURENCE
OF THE RESURRECTION

(1614-1691)

Nicholas Herman was born in Lorraine in 1614. We know little about his youth, but at the age of eighteen he was seized by a profound sense of the presence of God. He joined the army and was seriously wounded in battle. In 1640 he entered the Carmelite Order as a Discalced lay brother, taking the name Laurence of the Resurrection. He found religious life difficult, both with regard to externals and to his inner spirit. He worked first in the kitchen until his health compelled him to take up sandal-making. Gradually his fame spread in Paris and he was consulted by many, theologians and bishops, including the controversial Archbishop Fénelon, who found him 'rough by nature but delicate (or sensitive) in grace.'

He is most noted for the short book of his sayings and letters collected by a friend, a diocesan priest, Joseph de Beaufort and published as *The Practice of the Presence of God*. His 'method' was to recall consciously God's presence, using simple acts and prayers. In time this became habitual, and later mystical, as God seized him and gave him an almost continual awareness of the divine presence.

It is a big mistake to think that the period of mental prayer should be different from any other. We must be as closely united with God during our activities as we are during our times of prayer.

– Conversations 46

Neither finesse nor learning is required to approach God, only a heart resolved to devote itself exclusively to him, and to love him alone.

– Conversations 41

The practice of the presence of God is an application of our mind to God, or a remembrance of God present ... It would be appropriate for the beginner to formulate a few words interiorly, such as 'My God, I am completely yours,' or 'God of love, I love you with all my heart. ...' This practice of the presence of God, somewhat difficult in the beginning, secretly accomplishes marvellous effects in the soul, drawing abundant graces from the Lord, and when practised faithfully leads to this simple awareness, to this loving view of God present everywhere, which is the holiest, the surest, the easiest, and the most efficacious form of prayer.

– Spiritual Maxims 20, 30, 31

VEN JOHN OF ST SAMSON

(1571-1636)

John de Moulin was born in 1571 and became totally blind at the age of three. From 1601 until he entered Carmel in 1606 he lived generally in great poverty in Paris, spending many hours a day in church. He was a church organist for many years. Later, after Carmelite profession at Dol in Brittany, he transferred to the convent of Rennes and after a second novitiate Brother John became the heart of the Touraine reform of the Ancient Observance (O. Carm.). Outstanding in his love of sick and of poor people, he was one of the outstanding mystics of his age. In his writings John clearly draws on his own mystical experience, that is the knowledge and love which he has perceived in the passion and which is for his, and our, transformation and endless contemplation. He suffered much hardship in his life. His dying words were, 'With Christ I am tied to the cross.'

But, my Love and my Life, since your sacred passion caused and ran through you in infinite suffering, distress, contempt, confusion, dishonour, shame and disgrace until you died and expired on the cross in the sight and opprobrium of all, must we not be sure to contemplate from within the excellence of your infinite love, which is equal to yourself and not to go out from there, but to imitate continually from the angle of your most painful and laborious life your sufferings for the whole of our bodily life.

– Meditation on the Passion 20:178

All this love is very ravishing and admirable, and it astonishes heaven and earth, angels and men. But above what you have done there is a sea or impenetrable abyss, which is above all your other works. All that came after does not approach this communion of yourself in this most majestic and ineffable Sacrament given to us poor mortals, who are but dust and ashes. But in the Eucharist you have nevertheless elevated us, united us to your divinity and transformed us in it. However, this entire gift is received only in proportion to our love.

– Meditation on the Eucharist 16:144-145

Ibertus dei gra ierosolimi
tanne ecclie uocat̃ puarcha.
dilectis ĩ xp̃o filiis. B. ⁊ ceteis
heremitis/qui sb̃ eı obedientia
nr̃ fontem ĩ monte carmeli
morant̃ ĩ dn̄o salm̃. ⁊ sc̃i sp̃c
bn̄dictionem. cȝ ultifarie mr̃
tisqȝ modis sc̃i pr̃es ĩstitue
runt.q̃lit̃ quisqȝ ĩ d̃ct̃iqȝ ordi
ne fuit̃aul quemcũqȝ modũ
uite religiose uitȝ eleg̃it̃ ĩ
obsequio ihũ xp̃i uiuere debeat̃
⁊ eidem fidelit̃ de corde puro.
et bona ñsc̃ia deseruire. Ue
rum qa requiritis a nob̃.ut
ir̃ ꝓpositũ p̃r̃m.tradam̃ uo
bis uitȝ formulam q̃ teneɾe

Carmelite Rule (probably 14th century) MS 194 Trinity College, Dublin.

THE RULE OF
ST ALBERT OF JERUSALEM

COMMENTARY

1] The Carmelite *Rule* begins like a formal medieval letter with a salutation and a blessing. Albert, Patriarch of Jerusalem, greets the hermits living on Mount Carmel together with a leader. Albert's opening words would remind readers of one of the letters of St Paul. This leader is simply called 'B' in the text since his precise identity is unknown (cf chapter 22). The early Carmelites were dwelling near a spring on Mount Carmel, a mountain range, a place, from which they came to derive their name. In time both Mount Carmel and the spring near which the first Carmelites settled became powerful symbols for the Carmelite understanding of the spiritual journey as transformation in Christ.

2] The call to holiness is universal. No matter what our status in life we must be centred on Christ. Living in allegiance to Christ (see 2 Cor 10:5) took on feudal overtones in medieval times; it suggests that Christians are servants of Christ, belonging to him as their Lord and protector. But purity of heart becomes the key emphasis for Albert because it alone enables us to open up to God and helps us to come to see the world as if with his eyes (see *Catechism of the Catholic Church* 2519).

TEXT

1] Albert, called by the grace of God to be Patriarch of the Church of Jerusalem, greets his beloved sons in Christ, B, and the other hermits living in obedience to him near the spring on Mount Carmel: salvation in the Lord and the blessing of the Holy Spirit.

2] Many times and in different ways the holy Fathers have laid down that everyone – whatever be their state in life or the religious life chosen by them – should live in allegiance to Jesus Christ and serve him zealously with a pure heart and a good conscience.

3] The early Carmelites have taken the initiative in approaching Albert as the representative of ecclesiastical authority. They are concerned to consolidate their position, to plan for the future and, furthermore, to be of service to the wider Church community. Note how Albert is being asked to write them a rule (here called a 'way of life' or *formula vitae*) based on how the hermits were *already* living. There is, therefore, already a sense of the Carmelite *Rule* as a living text, the putting into words of a way of living (*propositum*), intended to inspire others to live the way of Carmel into the future.

4] The *Rule* proposes a particular model of leadership among Carmelites. A prior is to be elected and remains one of them, a first among equals. Carmelites are to pledge obedience to their prior. Ultimately such obedience is a sign of one's fidelity or allegiance to Christ, since later, in chapter 23, Carmelites are encouraged to honour their prior and 'rather than thinking about him, you are to look to Christ who set him as head over you'. The explicit reference to chastity and poverty as fulfilling (along with deeds) one's obedience to the prior was added in a later revision of the text.

3] Now then you have come to me seeking a formula of life according to your purpose, which you are to observe in the future.

4] The first thing I lay down is that you shall have a prior, one of yourselves, chosen by the unanimous consent of all, or of the greater and more mature part. All the others shall promise him obedience fulfilling it by deeds, as well as chastity and the renunciation of property.

5] 'The prior and the brothers' becomes a constant refrain throughout the *Rule* of Albert. Chapter 5 is a later addition to the text and witnesses to the expansion of the Carmelites in Europe. It makes provision for them to take up residence in solitary places or in other places given to them. All of this is at the discretion of the prior and the brothers who together discern the suitability of locations for foundation. It was this provision that enabled the hermit-brothers of Carmel to become friars, ultimately, 'a contemplative fraternity in the midst of the people.' (*Constitutions* 1995).

6] The key value of a life of *solitude* lived in community is made manifest in Albert's provision for a separate cell for each Carmelite. Once again, the prior and the brothers agree on the allocation of cells. Such a provision contrasts with those communities of monks who sleep in dormitories. The individual cell becomes a defining characteristic of the Carmelite way of life. For the Carmelite imagination the cell becomes a *locus* ('a place') for encounter with God.

5] You can take up places in solitary areas or in sites given to you, one suitable and convenient for your observance in the judgement of the prior and the brothers.

6] Moreover, taking account of the site you propose to occupy, all of you are to have separate cells; these are to be assigned by the prior himself with the agreement of the other brothers or the more mature of them.

7] Initially we know the early Carmelites lived strictly as hermits, taking meals in their individual cells. This later revision of Albert's text requires each Carmelite to eat in a common refectory. This is but one way in which individual Carmelites are called to move out beyond themselves and to share with others. And just as the Carmelite receives bodily nourishment in the common refectory, he also receives spiritual nourishment in listening, along with his brothers, to readings from scriptures. Bodily and spiritual nourishment go together.

8] This chapter is a mark of how seriously the early Carmelites took the allocation of an individual cell to each hermit. Even in the spiritual journey, the far-off hills are greener; a brother might think, if he had another cell, how much more satisfied and holy he could be.

9] Carmel is from the very beginning a place of welcome. The prior's cell is to be near the entrance so he can greet all those who come to visit, so he can receive pilgrims in a fitting manner and discern the initial suitability of those who wanted to join the brotherhood. Once again, the way of Carmel is both a journey within and a moving out from the centre.

7] You are, however, to eat in a common refectory what may have been given to you, listening together to a reading from holy scriptures, if this can conveniently be done.

8] No brother is permitted to change the place assigned to him or exchange with another, unless with the permission of the prior at the time.

9] The prior's cell shall be near the entrance to the place so that he may first meet those who come to the place and everything afterwards may be done as he wills and decides.

10] Chapter 10 clearly echoes Psalm 1: 'their delight is in the law of the Lord, and on his law they meditate day and night'. This chapter of the *Rule* expresses a key aim of the Carmelite life: that of praying unceasingly (see 1 Thess 5: 17). The idea of keeping vigilance is an echo of 1 Peter 4:7 and places the spiritual life of the Carmelite within the perspective of the return, or Second Coming, of Jesus. The injunction to remain in one's cell must, however, always be read alongside those chapters of the *Rule* which deal with fraternal life, with listening to the Word of God along with the brothers in the refectory, with the celebration of the Eucharist and with work. The cell, the oratory, the refectory and the ministry of welcome are all part of the Carmelite vision of a solitary life lived in common.

11] Chapter 11 of the *Rule* of Albert attests to the importance of the celebration of the Liturgy of the Hours in the daily life of the Carmelites. It makes practical provisions for those who are unable to do so, perhaps because of illiteracy. Commentators generally agree that at first the Psalms or Hours were probably celebrated by Carmelites individually in the privacy of their cell.

10] All are to remain in their cells or near them, meditating day and night on the law of the Lord and being vigilant in prayers, unless otherwise lawfully occupied.

11] Those who have learned to say the canonical hours with the clerics should do so according to the practice of the holy Fathers and the approved custom of the Church. Those who do not know the hours are to say the *Our Father* twenty-five times for the night office – except for Sunday and solemn feasts when this number is doubled, so that the *Our Father* is said fifty times. It is to said seven times for the morning Lauds and for the other Hours, except for Vespers when it must be said fifteen times.

12] The renunciation of property has already been mentioned (chapter 4). Here the importance of such renunciation is underlined. Goods held in common are to be distributed by the prior or his deputy. The *Rule* is sensitive to the fact that individuals may have different needs. The prior should, in other words, treat everyone according to their circumstances, but not necessarily in the same way. Some will always need more than others.

13] This is a later provision which reflects the fact that the hermits on Mount Carmel did need to travel, moving outwards from their settlement. The means are modest, unlike horses which were for the rich.

14] Chapter 14 of the *Rule* of Albert is a key text in the Carmelite tradition, emphasising as it does the centrality of the Eucharist. Here remaining in one's cell is balanced and complemented by gathering daily for Mass. We know from other sources that the early Carmelites named their oratory after Our Lady.

12] None of the brothers is to claim something as his own; everything is to be in common and is to be distributed to each one by the Prior – that is, the brother deputed by him to this office – having regard to the age and needs of each one.

13] You may have asses or mules according to your needs and some provision of animals or poultry.

14] An oratory is to be built as conveniently as possible in the midst of the cells; you are to gather daily in the morning for Mass, where this is convenient.

15] Chapter 15 points to two key elements of the Carmelite way: discernment and dialogue. Provision is made for regular meetings of the community to discuss its common aims, to address practical and spiritual matters as well as problematic behaviour on the part of the brothers. All this is to be accomplished in a spirit of open dialogue and in a spirit of charity.

16] The next two chapters of Albert's *Rule* deal with fasting and abstinence which is undertaken both as a penance and as a preparation for the celebration of major religious feasts. This practice was similar to that followed by other orders. Once again, a spirit of common sense prevails as Albert's *Rule* allows for exceptions. The statement: 'necessity has no law' is a standard expression of ancient Roman law.

17] The dispensation allowing for meat to be consumed while on a journey and while travelling at sea was added to Albert's *Rule* in 1247 and is further evidence of the expansion outwards of the Order. The wording of this chapter was borrowed from the Dominican Constitutions.

15] On Sundays, or other days if necessary, you shall discuss the welfare of the group and the salvation of souls; at this time excesses and faults of the brothers, if such come to light, are to be corrected in the middle way of charity.

16] You are to fast every day except Sundays from the feast of the Exaltation of the Cross until Easter Sunday, unless illness or bodily weakness, or other just cause counsels a lifting of the fast, since necessity has no law.

17] You are to abstain from meat, unless it is to be taken as a remedy for illness or bodily weakness. Since you must more frequently beg on journeys, in order not to burden your hosts you may eat food cooked with meat outside your own houses. At sea, however, meat may be eaten.

18] Chapter 18 sees the beginning of a new 'section' of the *Rule* of Albert wherein he spells out the implications of living a life in allegiance to Jesus Christ. For the Carmelite, living 'in allegiance to Jesus Christ' is envisaged in terms of a battle with the powers of evil both inside and outside ourselves. In this and succeeding chapters of the *Rule* there are clear echoes of the New Testament, particularly the letters of Paul. While the militaristic language and imagery would have resonated with the experience of the early Carmelites, living as they did in the era of the Crusades, here such imagery is given spiritual significance. Carmelites are to put on the amour of God to withstand the forces of evil (Eph 6:11, 13). Wearing God's armour is closely linked to the idea of living in allegiance to Jesus Christ. St Paul in 2 Cor 10:4-5 speaks of the 'arms of warfare' and 'walking in the footsteps of Jesus'. Representing the desert tradition, John Cassian, when questioned by a monk who complains he cannot master his thoughts and imaginings, uses the image of the soldier who puts on the armour of God to fight the battle of the Lord (*Collatio* 7:5). The image of the devil as a prowling lion is taken from 1 Peter 5:8.

18] Since human life on earth is a trial and all who want to live devotedly in Christ suffer persecution, your enemy the devil prowls about like a roaring lion seeking whom he might devour. You must then with all diligence put on the armour of God so that you may be able to stand up to the ambushes of the enemy.

19] Albert continues the theme of donning the armour of God which has six parts: the belt of chastity, the tunic of holy thoughts, the breastplate of justice, the shield of faith, the helmet of salvation, the sword of the spirit are based on Ephesians 6:10-17. First we should note that it is God's armour. All the armour is for protection except for one offensive weapon, the sword of the spirit. With God's armour our deepest human feelings are protected (belt of chastity). We can be attacked by evil and so we need the protection of holy thoughts. Justice will enable us to love, faith will protect us from what is not God. Salvation keeps us in the sphere of God. The helmet of salvation and the sword of the Spirit are both images taken from Ephesians 6:17.

19] Your loins are to be girded with the belt of chastity; your breast is to be protected by holy thoughts, for the scriptures says, holy thoughts will save you. Put on the breastplate of justice, so that you may love the Lord your God from your whole heart, your whole soul and your whole strength, and your neighbour as yourselves. In all things take up the shield of faith, with which you will be able to extinguish all the darts of the evil one; without faith, indeed, it is impossible to please God. The helmet of salvation is to be placed on your head, so that you may hope for salvation from the one Saviour, who saves his people from their sins. The sword of the Spirit, which is the word of God, is to dwell abundantly in your mouths and hearts. So whatever you have to do, is to be done in the word of the Lord.

20] The *Rule* of Carmel continues with an explicit reference to the second letter of St Paul to the Thessalonians. Here with the aid of Paul Albert insists that the hermits on Mount Carmel should engage in 'some work'. What does this entail? Paul's text and St Augustine's later interpretation of it put a clear emphasis on manual work (see his *De opere monachorum*, PL 40, 547-582). Undoubtedly the work of the early Carmelites on Mount Carmel was most probably manual. However, when they came to settle in Europe in 1247 it was likely they saw work in terms of the apostolate, in terms of preaching, teaching and caring for the sick and needy. Idleness was always a temptation for hermits, and so Albert repeats the hard quotation from Paul used in many monastic rules. For the remainder of the chapter Albert commends the vision of Paul in 2 Thessalonians to the early Carmelites. He says, echoing the words of Isaiah 30:21, 'This is a good and holy way: follow it.' Just before the end, in the penultimate sentence, we have a pre-echo of the succeeding section of the *Rule* which treats of silence.

20] You should do some work, so that the devil will always find you occupied and he may not through your idleness find some entrance to your souls.

In this matter you have both the teaching and the example of Blessed Paul the Apostle; Christ spoke through his mouth; he has been set up and given by God as a preacher and teacher of the nations in faith and truth; in following him you cannot go wrong.

In work and weariness, he said, we have been with you, working day and night so as not to be a burden to you; it was not as though we had no right, but we wished to give ourselves as a model for imitation. For when we were with you, we gave this precept: whoever is unwilling to work shall not eat. We have heard that there are restless people going around who do nothing. We condemn such people and implore them in the Lord Jesus Christ that working in silence they should earn their bread. This is a good and holy way: follow it.

21] The Carmelite *Rule* promotes silence for a number of reasons, some practical: gossip or chatter can lead to sin; night silence allows others to sleep. But the key point is that it promotes justice, that is, right relations with God and others. The Carmelite mystical tradition is unanimous in its insistence on silence. Associated with it are such ideas as happiness, calm, ease, quite, repose, serenity, tranquility. St Thérèse of Lisieux declared 'Silence is the language of heaven' (*Letters* 163: 20). Our modern world leaves little room for silence. Those who live in towns or near main roads become almost immune to the roar or steady hum of traffic. If the word 'silence' is not very frequent in the Bible, the corresponding word, 'listen' is everywhere. One point of being silent is to listen within to our own being, and more importantly to listen to God who may be speaking to us. The *Rule* of Albert lays down strict rules regarding the observation of complete silence on the part of Carmelites and emphasises just how injurious careless speech can be both to the person speaking and to others. The *Rule* is a call to each of us to rediscover the importance of silence in our lives.

21] The apostle therefore recommends silence, when he tells us to work in it; the prophet too testifies that silence is the promotion of justice; and again, in silence and in hope will be your strength. Therefore we lay down that from the recitation of Compline you are to maintain silence until after Prime the following day. At other times, though silence is not to be so strictly observed, you are to be diligent in avoiding much talking, since scripture states and experience likewise teaches, sin is not absent where there is much talking; also he who is careless in speech will experience evil, and the one who uses many words harms his soul. Again the Lord says in the gospel: an account will have to be given on the day of judgement for every vain word. Each of you is to weigh his words and have a proper restraint for his mouth, so that he may not stumble and fall through speech and his fall be irreparable and fatal. He is with the prophet to guard his ways so that he does not offend through the tongue. Silence, which is the promotion of justice, is to be diligently and carefully observed.

22] At this point Albert begins to draw the *Rule* to a close, once again along the lines of a letter. He address the prior by name 'Brother B'. Albert also looks to the future, pointing to the eventual succession that will take place with the appointment of a new prior. Referring to Matthew 20:26-27 he, once again, points to the radical and counter-cultural nature of the Carmelite understanding of leadership. In allegiance to Jesus Christ, and following his example, Carmelite leadership is one of service. The prior is first among equals and leads through service. This gospel ideal of authority is relevant still for Church and secular leaders today.

23] The relationship between the prior and the brothers is such that it reminds all concerned of the primary aim of the Carmelite way: to live in allegiance to Christ. The prior to whom the other Carmelites promise obedience and fidelity is not the ultimate focus. Christ is the foundation and focus of the Carmelite life.

22] You, Brother B, and whoever is appointed Prior after you, shall always keep in mind and practice what the Lord said in the gospel: Whoever wishes to be greater among you shall be your servant, and whoever wishes to be first must be your slave.

23] And you too, the other brothers, are humbly to honour your prior, and rather than thinking about him, you are to look to Christ who set him as head over you; he said to the leaders of the Church, whoever hears you hears me, and whoever despises you despises me. Thus you will not be judged guilty of contempt, but through obedience you will merit the reward of eternal life.

24] Albert's concluding chapter clearly echoes his own words in chapter 3: 'Now then you have come to me seeking a formula of life according to your purpose, which you are to observe in the future.' He has done what he set out to do. Albert's *Rule* ends with a reference to the parable of the Good Samaritan in Luke 10. Luke says: 'If you will have spent more, I shall reward you when I return' (Lk 10:35). Following this, Albert says: 'If anyone does more the Lord himself when he comes will repay him.' Albert concludes encouraging the Carmelites to use discretion or discernment. In the *Conferences* of Cassian, a fourth century monk quotes the Abbot Anthony as saying: 'Discernment is the mother, the guardian, and the guide of all the virtues.' (*Conferences* 2:4)

24] I have written these things briefly to you establishing a way of life for you, according to which you are to conduct yourselves. If anyone does more the Lord himself when he comes again will repay him. You are, however, to use discretion, which is the moderator of virtue.

Translation from *Ascending the Mountain: The Carmelite Rule Today* (The Columba Press, 2003)

Small chalice (ca 10 cm) 1571,
from Carmelite Friary, Knocktopher, Co Kilkenny.

CARMELITE REFLECTIONS

GOAL OF THE CARMELITE LIFE

THERE ARE MANY DESCRIPTIONS of holiness, even in the Christian tradition. The Carmelite *Rule* begins by referring to the 'many and various ways taught by the holy fathers' (n. 2). Ultimately all are different expressions, different emphases in the supreme command of loving God 'with all our heart, mind and strength and our neighbour as ourselves' (Mt 22:37-39).

In seeking holiness there are two big questions: what must I do? What must God do? There have been two heretical tendencies: relying too much on human effort (Pelagianism); leaving everything to God and dispensing with human striving (Quietism).

The whole spiritual journey is possible only with divine grace; God must help us at every stage. But at the beginning he helps us to get going and expects a lot of effort from us. This used to be called the ascetical way, which involves working hard at eliminating sin and cultivating virtue. Later God moves in to bring a person far beyond all human possibility. This was often called the mystical life.

The Carmelite saints are continually amazed that more people do not allow God to bring them to great holiness; people carelessly reject a pearl beyond price (see Mt 13:46).

The goal of this life is twofold. One part we acquire by our own effort and the exercise of the virtues, assisted by divine grace. This is to offer God a pure and holy heart, free from all stain of sin. We attain this goal when we are perfect … and hidden in that love which covers all offences (*Proverbs 10:12*).

The other goal of this life is granted to us as a free gift of God, namely, to taste somewhat in the heart and to experience in the mind the power of the divine presence and the sweetness of heavenly glory, not only after death but already in this mortal life.

– The Institutes of the First Monks (14th cent) 2:1

OUR LOVING GOD

THE SONG OF SONGS from the Old Testament has always been a favourite of Christian mystics down through the centuries. Several of the poems of St John of the Cross echo its language and imagery. The mystics understand this beautiful love poem as an expression and celebration of God's deep love for his people and for each individual person. Commenting on the poetry of St John, the Carmelite writer, John Welch, writes 'his understanding of our humanity is that we wake up in the middle of a love story. Someone has touched our hearts, wounding them, and making them ache for fulfilment.'

We tend to see the spiritual journey as our going off in search of God. The Carmelite mystics tell us, however, that the opposite is true – it is God who is searching for us – longing to share his love with us – longing to awaken a response of love within us.

God appears to hide from us not because he is indifferent to us but rather to awaken love within us – 'we love because he has first loved us' (1 John 4:1). John of the Cross calls this love a 'Living Flame' that both wounds and heals until the heart becomes one with the fire.

Although neo-paganism no longer wants love, history teaches us that, in spite of everything, we will conquer this neo-paganism with love. We shall not give up on love. Love will gain back for us the hearts of these pagans. Nature is stronger than theory; let theory condemn and reject love and call it weakness; the living witness of love will always renew the power which will conquer and capture the hearts of men.

– Carmelite Liturgy – Bl Titus Brandsma in response to Nazi ideology

Where there is no love, put love in and you will draw love out.

– St John of the Cross, Letter 24 (26)

THE WORD OF GOD

EVEN AT THE MOST CURSORY GLANCE the amount of scripture in the Carmelite *Rule* is quite striking. When Albert is not directly quoting scripture, the phrases he uses echo the Bible to such an extent that the *Rule* reads like one of the New Testament letters. Albert encourages the Carmelites to read or listen to the scriptures, to meditate or ponder on the scriptures, to pray using the scriptures, to allow the scriptures dwell in their hearts and to act on the basis of the scriptures. This approach to praying the scriptures is quite close to what is known as *Lectio divina*. Although the School of Carmel has many approaches to prayer, the method of *Lectio divina* seems particularly appropriate to it.

As Christians we know that Jesus Christ is the Word of God – the Word made flesh – the ultimate revelation of the Father. So the *Rule* is very Christocentric – that is centred on the person of Christ. The goal of reading and praying the scriptures is to allow our minds to be remade in the likeness of Christ and our hearts to be filled with his love. We are to become Christ-centred.

St John of the Cross says that the Father would say to us: 'I have already told you all things in my Word, my Son … in him I have spoken and revealed all, and in him you

will discover even more than you ask for and desire … I
have already spoken, answered, manifested and revealed
(all) to you, by giving him as your brother, companion,
master, ransom and reward.' (*Ascent of Mount Carmel*
2:22,5).

A Method of Lectio Divina

A scripture passage is chosen, perhaps from the weekday
or Sunday readings. One can begin with a short prayer
asking the guidance of the Holy Spirit.

- *Read* the passage slowly and attentively. Ask yourself
  what is the passage saying in itself?
- Read the passage again. *Reflect* on the passage. Ask
  yourself how it relates to your life and your experience
  – what is the word of God for you today?
- *Respond* prayerfully to the passage. Talk to Jesus as
  honestly as you can.
- *Rest* silently in the presence of God – responding with
  your heart to the passage and then allowing it to influ-
  ence your words and actions.

In conclusion one might choose a word or phrase from
the scriptures that sums up the passage for you and
which can be repeated afterwards. One can conclude with
a prayer of praise or thanksgiving for the prayer-time.

THE PRESENCE OF GOD

'A S THE LORD THE GOD OF ISRAEL LIVES, before whom I stand …' (1 Kgs 17:1). These words of the prophet Elijah as he confronts King Ahab have always caught the Carmelite imagination. Like Elijah we seek to have a constant awareness of God's presence – of the closeness of God to us. Of course we do not really have to put ourselves in the presence of God since God is always present: 'in him we live and move and have our being' (Acts. 17:28). However, we are often blind to God's presence and need to awaken a sense of that presence within us.

Perhaps the clearest expression of this element of Carmelite spirituality is to be found in the writings of Brother Laurence of the Resurrection (see p 54) whose simple and beautiful words on the practice of the presence of God have helped many grow in holiness. Laurence encourages us to turn frequently in our hearts to God who dwells within us. Even during our everyday activities we can pause for a moment and turn to God in loving prayer. Laurence advises us not to get discouraged when our thoughts wander to different concerns; we should just patiently bring them back to God.

A second point emphasised by the Rule is silence and recollection as a necessary condition for a life of prayer. Active recollection, by which we put ourselves and keep ourselves in the presence of God, has always been regarded as the essential preparation for communion with God in the mystic life. Just as the Prophet did not hear the voice of God in the storm, but in the gentle breeze, so the heart of the spiritual person must not be shaken by the storm but must listen for God's voice in the silence of its own interior.

– Bl Titus Brandsma, Carmelite Mysticism 19

PRAYER

PRAYER IS FOUND IN ALL RELIGIONS. It expresses profoundly my reality: I am a creature in need before a God who is both loving and powerful. The truth of my situation is expressed by the traditional four forms of prayer: adoration, thanksgiving, asking for mercy and forgiveness, and intercession. Prayer can be vocal – consisting usually of well established prayers, often composed by others; it can also be mental, in that I reflect before expressing my situation before God.

What is called vocal prayer must not just be mere words: I have to mean them. St Teresa of Avila warns: 'A prayer in which a person is not aware of whom he is speaking to, what he is asking, who it is who is asking and of whom, I do not call prayer at all however much the lips move' (*Interior Castle* 1:1, 7).

Mental prayer in particular brings me before God as I am. I need to reflect, especially with the help of scripture which draws me into knowing Jesus Christ, his life, his teaching and his attitudes. In prayer, I need to listen, to speak and to gaze. The point of prayer is to build a relationship in which I am changed in knowledge, desires, attitudes and behaviour in order to become a more committed disciple of Jesus Christ. Prayer is a gift for which we must pray; it is an art that we must practise; it is an indicator of the health of my relationship with God and others; it is a compass to direct me; it is a means and a test of my human authenticity.

For me, prayer is a surge of the heart; it is a simple look turned toward heaven, it is a cry of recognition and of love, embracing both trial and joy.

– St Thérèse of Lisieux, Story of a Soul MS C 25r quoted in Catechism of the Catholic Church 2558

Mental [contemplative] prayer in my opinion is nothing else than a close sharing between friends; it means taking time frequently to be alone with him who we know loves us.

– St Teresa of Avila, Life 8:5 quoted in Catechism of the Catholic Church 270.7

Elijah declared at his appearance to the Jews: 'As God lives in whose presence I stand.' Such is the foundation of his life of prayer. This living in the presence of God, this placing himself before the face of God is a characteristic which the children of Carmel have inherited from the great Prophet.

– Bl Titus Brandsma, Carmelite Mysticism 1

CONTEMPLATION

THE WORD 'CONTEMPLATION' can have many senses in religious writing. Its basic meaning involves the idea of looking, perhaps gazing. In the Carmelite tradition it is a gift of God, for which we may prepare especially in 'de-centering,' that is, making God and others, rather than ourselves, the centre of our lives and strivings. Purity of heart demands that we remove idols and sin from our lives, so as to be open to God, welcoming his grace and inner healing. Contemplation demands purity of heart. It is an encounter with God which transforms us.

In the tradition of John of the Cross, contemplation, sometimes in a dark form, begins when active discursive meditation is no longer fruitful or possible (*Ascent* 2, chs 13-17). In more recent Carmelite reflection, the inner process leading to the contemplative dimension helps us to acquire an attitude of openness to God's presence in life, teaches us to see the world with God's eyes, and inspires us to seek, recognise, love and serve God in those around us (*Carmelite Formation* (2000) n. 24).

Dark contemplation brings the soul closer to God … it safeguards and cares for the soul. Because of their weakness, individuals feel thick darkness and more profound obscurity the closer they come to God, just as they would feel greater darkness and pain, because of the weakness and impurity of their eyes, the closer they approached the immense brilliance of the sun.

– St John of the Cross, Dark Night 2: 16, 11

Contemplation is the inner journey of Carmelites, arising out of the free initiative of God, who touches and transforms us, leading towards unity in love with him, raising us up so that we may enjoy his gratuitous love and living in his loving presence. It is a transforming experience of the overpowering love of God. This love empties us of our limited and imperfect human ways of thinking, loving and behaving, transforming them into divine ways.

– Carmelite Constitutions (1995) 17

INNER JOURNEY

THE CARMELITE SEEKS GOD. The paradox, of course, is that before we seek God, the Trinity has already sought after us. Our seeking is a response to having been loved and found. It is a movement from where we are towards God. Its symbols are varied: finding a ladder, climbing a mountain, going on a journey, embarking on a pilgrimage, setting out on a voyage.

The most common Carmelite symbol is, however, the journey inwards; not a search for ourselves, or for personal authenticity, but a search for God who dwells within us. St Teresa of Avila saw our spiritual being as composed of seven rooms (she also called them mansions), which we enter in turn on the inward journey to God who dwells at the centre of our being. She further remarks that the way of entry is prayer (*Interior Castle* 2:1, 11). She also warns: 'In my opinion we shall never completely know ourselves if we don't strive to know God. By gazing at his grandeur, we get in touch with our own lowliness; by looking at his purity, we shall see our own filth; by pondering his humility, we shall see how far we are from being humble' (*Interior Castle* 1:2, 9).

'The kingdom of God is within you.' A while ago God invited us to remain in him, to live spiritually in his glorious heritage (see Luke 17:21; Eph 1:18), and he reveals to us that we do not have to go out of ourselves to find him: 'The Kingdom of God is within.'

– Bl Elizabeth of the Trinity, Heaven in Faith 2:5

O you who are so anxious to know the dwelling place of your Beloved so that you may go in search of him and be united with him, now we are telling you that you yourself are his dwelling and his secret room and hiding place. There is reason for you to be elated and joyful in seeing that all your good and hope is so close as to be within you, or better, that you cannot be without him. 'Behold,' exclaims the Bridegroom, 'the kingdom of God is within you' (Luke 17:21). And his servant, the apostle St Paul declares, 'You are the temple of God' (2 Cor 6:16).

– St John of the Cross, Spiritual Canticle 1:7

Jesus cannot dwell in half a heart.

– St Thérèse of Lisieux, Letter 102

TRANSFORMATION

TRANSFORMATION IS A RICHER WORD than change; it suggests that we are to be different. It is a favourite theme of Carmelite writers. Once again we have to be careful not to depend on preconceived meanings or what we might find in a dictionary. Spiritual terms become fixed and intelligible by the way they are used and by the context in which we find them. Transformation happens at several levels.

A first level might also be called conversion. God's grace helps us to see that in some ways we are unwell before him and in our lives. The scriptures point out to us various areas which are harmful and crucial positive attitudes to adopt. This will involve turning around, or letting idols go, or being serious about small sins … There are many such expressions. 'Daily conversion to the gospel is essential if we are to remain faithful to our vocation' (*Carmelite Constitutions* (1995) 46).

A second level is a further work of God's grace that conforms us to Jesus Christ. We have to be de-centered from selfishness towards seeking and serving God and others. This involves giving up what is damaging or useless to us by moving into greater authenticity or wholeness in our lives, as we hear Jesus saying, 'I came that they may have life and have it to the full' (John 10:10).

The final transformation before death is by divine self-communication: the Father, Son and Holy Spirit communicate themselves to us, and bring us into union with them. Carmelite spirituality takes up a theme from the Eastern Churches, that is, deification, so that we share in the divine nature (see 2 Pet 1:4).

Although transformation in this life can be what it was in St Paul (see Gal 2:29 'it is no longer I who live, but it is Christ who lives in me'), it still cannot be perfect and complete, even though the soul reaches such transformation of love as is found in the spiritual marriage, the highest state attainable on this earth. Everything can be called a sketch of love compared with that perfect image, the transformation in glory. Yet the attainment of such a sketch of transformation in this life is a very great blessing, for with this transformation the Beloved is well pleased.

– St John of the Cross, Spiritual Canticle 12:8

NIGHT

THOSE WHO LIVE IN CITIES and towns may rarely experience real night or darkness; they may seldom see the stars. The only way that they can obtain a sense of night is, perhaps, during a power failure when they stumble around an otherwise familiar room. Night can have its own fears; often young children and sick people can be afraid of the coming darkness.

Night in the Bible has both fascination and danger. The Israelite trusts in God for protection during the night: 'You will not feel the terror of the night … or the pestilence that stalks in darkness' (Ps 91:5-6). The night is the time of temptation, when sin comes more easily. It is also a time of grace: 'I bless the Lord who gives me counsel, who even at night directs my heart' (Ps 16:7).

Walking in darkness is an image of sin. Paul tells us: 'The night is far gone, the day is near. Let us then lay aside the works of darkness and put on the armour of light; let us live honourably as in the day' (Rom 13:12-13). The Christian must remember that Jesus is the 'true light' (Jn 1:9), 'the light of the world' (Jn 8:12; 9:5).

The Carmelite tradition takes up the rich night imagery of the Bible and adds another insight, that is, the process of transformation can be likened to night.

One dark night,
Fired with love's urgent longings
– Ah the sheer grace –
I went out unseen,
My house being now all stilled …

In darkness and secure,
By the secret ladder disguised
– Ah the sheer grace –
In darkness and concealment,
My house being now all stilled …

O guiding night!
O night more lovely than the dawn!
O night that has united
The lover with His beloved,
Transforming the beloved in her lover.

– St John of the Cross, from the poem 'One Dark Night'

I must immerse myself in the 'sacred darkness' by putting all my powers in darkness and emptiness; then I will meet my Master, and 'the light that surrounds him like a cloak' will surround me also … What does it matter to the soul that is absorbed in recollection of the light which these words create in it, whether it feels or does not feel, whether it is in darkness or light, whether it enjoys or does not enjoy.

– Bl Elizabeth of the Trinity, Last Retreat 4:10 and 11

DESERT

MOUNT CARMEL WAS A PLACE of solitude where the first Carmelites could devote their lives to prayer. The image of the desert or the wilderness as a place of solitude subsequently became important in Carmelite spirituality. Our experience of solitude can be very mixed. The desert can be a place of refuge – an escape from the noise and stresses of everyday life, giving us space to rest and become aware of God's closeness to us. However, it often happens that no sooner have we left the noise and distractions of everyday life than a thousand inner voices seem to clamour for our attention – memories, unresolved conflicts, hurts, anxieties and so on. The desert can be a dangerous place where we feel lost and alone and we become almost unbearably aware of our frailty and sin, our deepest desires, the hunger of our hearts. In the desert, moreover, people have to travel light leaving behind comforts. The *Rule* of St Albert seeks to guide us through the deserts of our lives – to allow God to transform them into places of beauty and growth. The message of Carmel is not to run away from the desert but to turn more and more in trust to God who transforms the desert into a garden.

[For the first Carmelites] the desert was more than a physical reality; it was a place of the heart. It was the context in which could be lived the commitment to focus one's being on God alone. They have chosen to follow Jesus Christ, who denied himself and emptied himself to the point of dying naked on the cross. People of pure faith, they awaited the gift of new and eternal life, fruit of the Lord's resurrection. The desert, a place of solitude and aridity, blooms and becomes the place where the experience of God's liberating presence builds community and inspires us to service. In the footsteps of the first Carmelite hermits, we too journey through the desert, which develops our contemplative dimension. This requires self-abandonment to a gradual process of emptying and stripping ourselves, so that we may be clothed in Christ and filled with God.

– Carmelite Formation (2000), 27

COMMUNITY

EVER SINCE THE FIRST HERMITS on Mount Carmel requested a way of life from St Albert, community has been an important element of the Carmelite charism. The first Carmelites were inspired by the portrait of the early Church in Jerusalem in the Acts of the Apostles. They were gathered together on the basis of the Apostles' preaching, sharing, the Eucharist and prayer (see 2:42). Now 'the whole group of those who believed were of one heart and soul, and nobody claimed private ownership, but everything was held in common' (4:32).

St Teresa of Avila wanted her communities to be places where 'all must be friends, all must be loved, all must be held dear, all must be helped' (*Way of Perfection* 4:7).

At a time when the sense of community seems to be breaking down in many societies, Carmelites feel a special call to work together to build up communities of various kinds in the Church and society, and to encourage people to come together.

This is the challenge. Called to live in community, we have to make our communities such that they are a real proof that community is possible. We are talking about community which is born out of listening to the Word of God, and so humanises its members, brings people together despite their differences and is thus a true presence of the gospel. In this way our communities will become signs of hope which will cause the poor to say about us what the widow of Zarepta said about Elijah, 'Now I know that you are a man of God and the word of God is in your mouth' (1 Kgs 17:24).

– Letter of Prior General and Superior General of Carmelites, John Malley, O.Carm and Camillo Maccise, OCD, 1992

SERVICE

ALTHOUGH THEIR PRIMARY FOCUS was on prayer, the life of the early hermits on Mount Carmel was not without an element of service. Being only a few miles from a main pilgrim road, they were able to provide sanctuary and hospitality for those on the way to Jerusalem. When they had to migrate to Europe, Carmelites quickly adopted the so-called 'mixed life' of the mendicant orders such as Dominicans and Franciscans and Augustinians.

There would be much tension between the active life of service and the contemplative life of prayer. But Carmelites, even contemplative nuns, always try to hold together in their lives the biblical figures of Martha and Mary (see Luke 10:38-42). In recent years many Carmelite authors avoid placing service and contemplation in a hierarchy. These instead interact: prayer leads to service; service feeds prayer; both are expressions of a higher reality which is the commandment to love taught by Jesus (see Mt 22:37-38).

Thérèse of Lisieux expressed the interaction of service and contemplation when she realised that her vocation was to be 'love in the heart of the Church.'

In prayer we open ourselves to God, who, by his actions, gradually transforms us through all the great and small events of our lives. This process of transformation enables us to enter into and sustain authentic relationships; it makes us willing to serve, capable of compassion and of solidarity, and gives us the ability to bring before the Father the aspirations, the anguish, the hopes and the cries of the people.

Fraternity is the testing ground of the authenticity of the transformation which is taking place within us. We discover that we are brothers and sisters journeying towards the one Father, sharing the gifts of the Spirit and supporting one another through the hardships of the journey.

From the free and disinterested service which only the contemplative can give, we receive unexpected assistance in our spiritual journey; this helps us to grow in openness to the action of the Spirit, and to allow ourselves to be sent out again and again, constantly renewed, to serve our sisters and brothers.

– Carmelite Formation (2000) n. 23

WORKS OF JUSTICE

LOVE FOR OTHERS has always been a Christian imperative (see Mt 22:39): 'I was hungry and you gave me to eat … thirsty … stranger … naked … sick … in prison' (See Mt 25:31-46). Carmelites like St Andrew Corsini (d. 1374), St John of the Cross and Bl Titus Brandsma were noted for their charity and love of the poor.

In the 1960s people became aware that there are deep problems in society that cannot be solved by individual or institutional acts of charity. There is a profound injustice, a 'dis-grace,' in society that calls for a graced response from Christians. Firstly in Latin America, then elsewhere, theologians and pastoral workers saw not just poverty, but oppression and a marginalisation of people that was not merely financial but based on other grounds such as race, culture or gender. Turning to the scriptures they found evidence of a God who cares for his people also in this world, a God who demands justice and liberation of the oppressed. From the 1970s the Carmelite Order has seen as an element of its prophetic mission involvement in the struggle for human dignity, basic human needs and freedom.

Each place will provide different challenges and opportunities. A key issue is not so much providing immediate assistance or hand-outs, but working with the poor and marginalised, learning from them and enabling them to be ministers of their own liberation.

We live in a world full of injustice and disquiet. It is our duty to contribute to an understanding of the causes of these evils; to be in solidarity with the sufferings of those who are marginalised; to share in their struggle for justice and peace; and to fight for their total liberation, helping them to fulfil their desire for a decent life. We cannot turn a deaf ear to the cry of the oppressed who plead for justice. We must hear and interpret reality from the perspective of the poor – of those who are oppressed by the economic and political systems which today govern humanity. Social reality challenges us. Attentive to the cry of the poor, and faithful to the gospel, we must take our stand with them, making an option for the 'little ones'. There is a growing desire within the Order to choose solidarity with the 'little ones' of history, to bring to our brothers and sisters a word of hope and salvation from their midst, more by our lives than by our words ... We recommend this option for the poor, because it is in keeping with the charism of the Order.

– Carmelite Constitutions (1995) nn. 111-114

St Mary Magdelen de'Pazzi Window in the Carmelite Church, Kinsale, Co Cork.

PRAYERS
FROM THE TRADITION

MARY MOTHER OF CARMEL

Dear Mother of Carmel,
we pray you to commend
to your divine Son
all the cares and anxieties
of those who have asked our prayers:
help and restore those suffering
in body or mind,
pity those who are tried
by ill-health and disease,
give them light in darkness,
and in your great compassion
for the afflicted and unhappy
lead them close to the strength
of Jesus Christ, your Son our Lord. Amen.

We commend to your safe keeping,
Our Lady of Carmel,
our parents, relatives, and friends,
and all those who have done good for us
for the sake of your holy name;
guard them from temptation and surprise,
and keep them from evil and misfortune.

SPLENDOUR OF CARMEL

O most Blessed and Immaculate Virgin,
Ornament and Splendour of Carmel,
you regard with special kindness those
who wear your blessed habit,
look down kindly on me and cover me
with the mantle of your special protection.
Strengthen my weakness with your power;
enlighten the darkness of my mind with your wisdom;
increase in me faith, hope and charity.
Adorn my soul with such graces and virtues
that I may be pleasing to your Divine Son and to you.
Assist me in life, console me in death,
and present me to the Most Holy Trinity
as your devoted servant and child,
so that I may eternally bless and praise you
in paradise. Amen.

VERSES TO OUR LADY OF MOUNT CARMEL

Blessed Virgin of Mount Carmel:
>be our constant hope.

Mary, perfect disciple of the Lord:
>make us also faithful to him.

Mary, Flower of Carmel:
>fill us with your joy.

Virgin Mary, Beauty of Carmel:
>smile upon your family.

Sweet Mother of Carmel:
>accept me as your child.

Mary, Mother beyond compare:
>remember your children forever.

Holy Virgin, Star of the Sea:
>be our Beacon of Light.

Protecting Veil:
>shelter us in the mantle of your love.

Mary conceived without sin{
>pray for us who have recourse to you.

BEFORE AN ICON OF OUR LADY OF MOUNT CARMEL

O God,
you have given us Mary as our Mother
and, through the Order of Carmel,
we learn to call her Sister.
May we imitate her goodness and faith,
and be ever joyful in the wonderful things
you have done for us.
May Mary watch over and protect us
on our pilgrim way to your holy mountain,
Christ the Lord.
We make our prayer through the same Christ, our Lord.
Amen.

– Terenure College

THE PROPHET ELIJAH

Elijah was a human being like us,
and he prayed fervently that it might not rain;
and for three years and six months
it did not rain on earth.

Then he prayed again and the heavens gave rain
and the earth was fruitful.
By the word of God he closed up the heavens
and brought down fire three times from heaven.

(pause for reflection)

Let us pray:
Almighty God you raised up Elijah,
your prophet and our Father,
in a fiery chariot to heaven before he might die;
we ask you that while we still live
our hearts may be lifted up to eternal things
and that we may rejoice with him
at the resurrection of the just.
We ask this through Christ our Lord. Amen.

– from the ancient Carmelite liturgy

SAINT JOSEPH

This is the faithful and prudent servant
whom the Lord placed over his family.

Glory and riches are in his house
and his justice will remain forever.

(pause for reflection)

Let us pray:
O God in your wonderful providence you chose
Blessed Joseph as the husband of the most holy
Mother of God.
As we venerate this patron on earth,
may we have his intercession in heaven.
Who live and reign for ever and ever. Amen

– from the ancient Carmelite liturgy

St Joseph the Worker Window in Carmelite Church, Moate, Co Westmeath.

SAINT ANNE

Saint Anne, Mother of the Blessed Virgin,
filled with compassion for all who call on you
and particularly for those who suffer,
we come before you asking your help.
Intercede for us in your kindness.
Obtain for us the final grace
of beholding God face to face,
and with you and Mary and all the saints
praising and loving him eternally. Amen.

PRAYER TO THE GUARDIAN ANGEL

Angel of God, my guardian dear,
to whom God's love commits me here,
ever this day be at my side
to light and guard, to rule and guide. Amen

Approved Pius VI (1795)

SALVE REGINA

Hail, Holy Queen, Mother of Mercy,
hail our life, our sweetness and our hope.
To you do we cry poor banished children of Eve:
to you do we send up our sighs,
mourning and weeping in this valley of tears.
Turn then most gracious advocate,
your eyes of mercy towards us;
and after this our exile,
show unto us the
blessed fruit of your womb, Jesus.
O clement, O loving, O sweet Virgin Mary.

V. Pray for us, O Holy Mother of God.
R. That we may be made worthy
   of the promises of Christ.

Protect your servants, Lord, and keep us in peace.
As we trust in the intercession of the
Blessed Virgin Mary and all the saints,
keep us safe from every danger
and bring us to everlasting life
through Christ our Lord. Amen.

REGINA CAELI

Queen of heaven, rejoice, alleluia!
for he whom you were worthy to bear, alleluia!
has risen as he said, alleluia!
Pray for us to God, alleluia!

V. Rejoice and be glad, O Virgin Mary.
R. For the Lord has risen indeed; Alleluia.

O God, you gave joy to your family through the resurrection
of your Son, grant we beseech you that through his
Mother, the Virgin Mary we may obtain the joys of
everlasting life; through the same Jesus Christ our Lord
Amen.

The Regina Caeli is said instead of the Angelus during
Eastertide

PRAYER ON PUTTING ON A SCAPULAR

In the name of the Father who is in heaven
and of the Son who suffered the passion,
the Holy Spirit who strengthens me
and the Glorious Virgin who is my guide.

May we rise with God and may God rise with us,
may the cross of the nine angels be from sole to head,
the Scapular of Mary round us,
and behind us the sins of the world.

In ainm an Athar atá ar neamh
agus an Mhic a d'fhulaing an phian,
an Spioraid Naoimh atá de mo neartú,
is an Mhaighdean ghlórmhar atá do mo threorú. Amen.

Go n-éirí sinn le Dia agus go n-éirí Dia linn,
cros na naoi n-aingeal faoinár mbonn go dtí ár mbaithis,
Scaball Mhuire faoinár gcom
Agus ár gcúl le peacaí an domhain.
from Ár bPaidreacha Dúchais, Diarmuid Ó Laoghaire (FÁS)

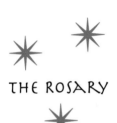

THE ROSARY

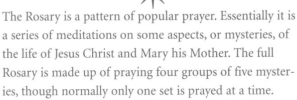

The Rosary is a pattern of popular prayer. Essentially it is a series of meditations on some aspects, or mysteries, of the life of Jesus Christ and Mary his Mother. The full Rosary is made up of praying four groups of five mysteries, though normally only one set is prayed at a time. Meditation on each mystery is accompanied by saying:

> The Lord's Prayer
> The Hail Mary (ten times)
> Glory be to the Father ...

Periods of silence are an important part of praying the Rosary.

The Mysteries of the Rosary

Joyful Mysteries
The Annunciation of the Lord
The Visitation of the Virgin Mary to her cousin Elizabeth
The Birth of the Lord
The Presentation of Jesus in the Temple
The Finding of the Child Jesus in the Temple.

Mysteries of Light
The Baptism of Jesus in the River Jordan
The Sign at the Wedding Feast in Cana

The Preaching of the Kingdom
The Transfiguration
The Institution of the Eucharist.

Sorrowful Mysteries
The Agony in the Garden
The Scourging at the Pillar
The Crowning with Thorns
The Carrying of the Cross
The Crucifixion of the Lord.

Glorious Mysteries
The Resurrection of the Lord
The Ascension of the Lord
The Coming of the Holy Spirit at Pentecost
The Assumption of the Virgin Mary into Heaven
The Coronation of Mary as Queen of Heaven.

*The scourging from the Stations of the Cross batik by Bernadette Madden
in St Colmcille's Church, Knocklyon, Dublin.*

TRADITIONAL CARMELITE TABLE PRAYERS

Before the meal

All: The eyes of all look to you and you give them their food in due time. You open wide your hand and you grant the desires of all who live.

Our Father…

Leader: Bless us Lord and these your gifts which of your goodness we are about to receive. Through Christ our Lord. Amen.

After the meal

All: May all your works glorify you, O Lord, and all your saints give you praise. Glory be to the Father …

Leader: We give you thanks, Almighty God, for all your benefits. Who live and reign for ever and ever.

All: Amen

Leader: May it please you, O Lord, to reward with eternal life all who have been good to us for your name's sake.

All: Amen.

All: Hail Mary …

May the souls of the faithful departed, through the mercy of God, rest in peace. Amen.

Leader: Let us bless the Lord.

All: Thanks be to God.

For liturgical seasons

Advent

Before the meal: The Lord is coming alleluia. Our Father …
After the meal: The Lord is coming alleluia. Glory be to the Father …

Christmas

Before the meal: The Word became flesh alleluia
and dwelt among us alleluia. Our Father …
After the meal: The Word became flesh alleluia
and dwelt among us alleluia. Glory be to the Father …

Lenten time

Before: Show us your mercy, Lord, and grant us your salvation. Our Father …
After: Show us your mercy, Lord, and grant us your salvation. Glory be to the Father …

Easter time

Before: The Lord is truly risen alleluia. Let us rejoice and be glad alleluia. Our Father …
After: The Lord is truly risen alleluia. Let us rejoice and be glad alleluia. Glory be to the Father …

Pentecost

Before: The Spirit of the Lord fills the whole earth alleluia. Our Father …
After: The Spirit of the Lord fills the whole earth alleluia. Glory be to the Father …

A PRAYER AT NIGHT

Dear Lord, I've tried all day to please you,
But while my eyes had light to see
By the burning of the sun,
There was no virtue in my moiling.
For all my busy labour, now I lie here
Weary, empty-handed.
And yet this day has not been wasted,
Nor its hours vain,
For, Jesus, here at last I give you perfect service.
That which I could not do
In the clear light of the sun and of a conscious mind
Is smoothly done here in the night
When I know it not.
For now I bid my heart be faithful,
And its every beat rings true to you,
Nor is there any law
By which it does that which it wills not.
Now I have lost all pride
And care for outward show,
And am become in truth a child with tousled hair.
Now, Lord, at last my eyes have done with foolish longing,
And my lips with falsehood,
My hands with vain contriving,
And my feet are still.

– Joachim Smet, O. Carm.

ST THÉRÈSE

St Thérèse of the Child Jesus
and of the Holy Face:
Teach us to follow your way
of confidence and trust.
Help us to realise that
a Father's love watches over us
each day of our lives.
Obtain for us the light to see,
in sorrow as in joy,
in trials as in peace,
the loving hand of our Father.
Give us your own faith and trust,
so that we may walk in darkness,
as in the light, holding fast
to the way of love,
knowing as you did,
that everything is a grace.

Tallow Carmel

Jesus, you are my only love.
*– Etched on the cell door of St Thérèse
and recited by her during her trial of faith.*

FOR THE CARMELITE FAMILY

Ever loving God,
renew the gift of the Holy Spirit
within the Carmelite Family
as we seek to live following
in the footsteps of Jesus Christ.
Teach us, like Mary, to contemplate your wisdom.
Fill us, like Elijah, with zeal for your glory.
Inspire us like, Simon Stock,
to ponder your will in times of change.
Like Teresa, John, Thérèse and Titus
may we live always in your presence,
and make us prophets of your Kingdom.
May our lives of prayer, community and service
be a sign to the world that God lives,
in whose presence we stand.
We ask these things in Jesus' name.
Amen.

FOR THE SICK

Lord Jesus, who went about doing good
and healing all,
we ask you to bless your friends who are sick.
Give them strength in body, courage in spirit,
and patience with pain.
Let them recover their health,
so that, restored to the Christian community,
they may joyfully praise your name.
For you live and reign for ever and ever. Amen.

St Albert of Trapani from the Rose Window in White Abbey, Kildare.

FOR VOCATIONS AND THE MISSIONS

O God, who willed that all people should be saved
and come to a knowledge of the truth,
send, we ask you, labourers into your harvest
and enable them to speak your word with confidence,
so that your good news may run and be made plain,
and that all people should know you,
the One, True God, and him whom you have sent,
Jesus Christ, your Son, our Lord. Amen.

I praise, bless and thank you Lord.
You know that it is always difficult to pull myself away
from the concerns and challenges that occupy my mind.
I want to listen to you, Lord.
Help me to listen like Mary and Elijah
and to overcome my reluctance to respond to your call.
I trust in your help to assist me
in taking the journey that you desire me to make.
Amen.

FOR DISCERNMENT

O God, you search me and you know me,
you know my resting and my rising,
you discern my purpose from afar.
All my ways lie open to you.
You have blessed me with many gifts and talents.
Grant me the wisdom to know how best
to use them for the glory of your name.
Grant me the desire to reach out
and embrace all people with your love,
to be your hands in the world.
Grant me the courage to echo in my life
the Yes of Mary and the passionate fidelity
of Elijah your prophet.
Help me to see in myself what you see,
and give me the courage to follow
wherever you may lead.
Through Jesus Christ Our Lord. Amen.

PRAYER OF BL ELIZABETH OF THE TRINITY

O my God, Trinity whom I adore; help me to forget myself entirely that I may be established in you as still and as peaceful as if my soul were already in eternity. May nothing trouble my peace or make me leave you, O my Unchanging One, but may each minute carry me further into the depths of your mystery. Give peace to my soul; make it your heaven, your beloved dwelling and your resting place. May I never leave you there alone but be wholly present, my faith wholly vigilant, wholly adoring, and wholly surrendered to your creative Action.

O my beloved Christ, crucified by love, I wish to be a bride for your Heart; I wish to cover you with glory; I wish to love you ... even unto death! But I feel my weakness, and I ask you to 'clothe me with yourself', to identify my soul with all the movements of your Soul, to overwhelm me, to possess me, to substitute yourself for me that my life may be but a radiance of your Life. Come into me as Adorer, as Restorer, as Saviour.

O Eternal Word, Word of my God, I want to spend my life in listening to you, to become wholly teachable that I may learn all from you. Then, through all nights, all voids, all helplessness, I want to gaze on you always and remain in your great light. O my beloved Star, so fascinate me that I may not withdraw from your radiance.

O consuming Fire, Spirit of Love, 'come upon me', and create in my soul a kind of incarnation of the Word: that I may be another humanity for him in which he can renew his whole Mystery. And you, O Father, bend lovingly over your poor little creature; 'cover her with your shadow', seeing in her only the 'Beloved in whom you are well pleased'.

O my Three, my All, my Beatitude, infinite Solitude, Immensity in which I lose myself, I surrender myself to you as your prey. Bury yourself in me that I may bury myself in you until I depart to contemplate in your light the abyss of your greatness.

Detail from Main Altar in Church of the Nativity, Beaumont, Dublin.

NIGHT PRAYER WITH MARY
OUR MOTHER AND SISTER

Window of Our Lady of Mount Carmel, Harry Clarke Studios,
in Gort Muire Chapel, Ballinteer, Dublin.

NIGHT PRAYER WITH MARY OUR MOTHER AND SISTER

In the name of the Father, and of the Son, and of the Holy Spirit. Amen.

Reflect on the past day and then say:

Have mercy on me, God, in your kindness.
In your compassion blot out my offence.
O wash me more and more from my guilt
And cleanse me from my sin.

May the almighty and merciful Lord grant me pardon and forgiveness and the grace and comfort of the Holy Spirit. Amen.

Hymn
For Mary, Mother of the Lord,
God's holy name be praised,
Who first the Son of God adored
As on her child she gazed.

The angel Gabriel brought the word
She should Christ's mother be;
Our Lady, handmaid of the Lord,
Made answer willingly.

The heavenly call she thus obeyed,
And so God's will was done;

The second Eve love's answer made
Which our redemption won.

Hail, Mary, you are full of grace,
Above all women blest;
Blest in your Son, whom your embrace
In birth and death confessed.

– J. R. Peacey

Choose psalm A or B

A Psalm 31 (30)
In you, O Lord, I take refuge.
Let me never be put to shame.
In your justice, set me free,
hear me and speedily rescue me.

Be a rock of refuge for me,
a mighty stronghold to save me,
for you are my rock, my stronghold.
For your name's sake, lead me and guide me.

Release me from the snares they have hidden
for you are my refuge, Lord.
Into your hands I commend my spirit,
It is you who will redeem me, Lord.

O God of truth, you detest
those who worship false and empty gods.
As for me, I trust in the Lord:
let me be glad and rejoice in your love.

You who have seen my affliction
and taken heed of my soul's distress,

have not handed me over to the enemy,
but set my feet at large.
Glory be …

or
B Psalm 113 (112)
Praise, O servants of the Lord,
praise the name of the Lord!
May the name of the Lord be blessed
both now and for evermore!
From the rising of the sun to its setting
praised be the name of the Lord!

High above all nations is the Lord,
above the heavens his glory.
Who is like the Lord, our God,
who has risen on high to his throne
yet stoops from the heights to look down,
to look down upon heaven and earth?

From the dust he lifts up the lowly,
from his misery he raises the poor
to set him in the company of princes,
yes, with the princes of his people.
To the childless wife he a gives a home
and gladdens her heart with children.
Glory be …

Scriptures Reading A or B
A Acts 1:14
With one accord the apostles devoted themselves to
prayer, together with Mary the mother of Jesus, and his
brothers.

B Galatians 4:4-5

When the fullness of time had come, God sent his Son, born of a woman, born under the law, in order to redeem those who were under the law, so that we might receive adoption as sons and daughters.

Short Responsory

R The Word was made flesh, he lived among us and we saw his glory.

V The glory that is his as the only Son of the Father.

R Glory be to the Father and to the Son
    and to the Holy Spirit.

R The Word was made flesh and lived among us and we saw his glory.

Nunc Dimittis *Canticle of Luke 2:29-32*

At last, all powerful Master,
you give leave to your servant
to go in peace, according to your promise.

For my eyes have seen your salvation
which you have prepared for all nations,
the light to enlighten the Gentiles
and give glory to Israel, your people.
Glory be …

Almighty God and Father, who received the Blessed Virgin into your eternal presence, grant that through her intercession we may rest secure this night and rise refreshed to praise your glory.
Through Christ our Lord. Amen.

Flower of Carmel,
Tall vine, blossom laden,
Splendour of heaven,
Child bearing, yet maiden,
None equals thee.

Mother so tender,
Whom no man didst know,
On Carmel's children
Your favour bestow,
Star of the Sea!

Concluding Prayer

Let us pray:
Lord, by a special privilege, you adorned the Order of
Carmel with the name of your Mother, the most glorious
Virgin Mary:
As we faithfully remember this honour, grant that in
these days we may receive her protection, and in the days
to come be brought, through her prayers, to the joy of
heaven. We ask this of you who live and reign for ever
and ever.
Amen.

Blessing

May Mary our mother and sister
help us in every trial and danger,
and may God grant us peace and everlasting life.
Amen.

— Text: Gort Muire

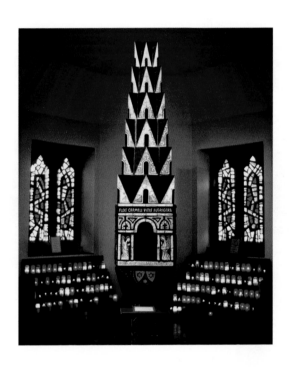

Reliquary of St Simon Stock by Adam Kossowski at The Friars, Aylesford, Kent.

*Church at Avila Mission, Zimbabwe, designed and built
by Senan Egan O. Carm (d. 1992).*

THE TRADITION LIVES

THE TRADITION LIVES

The Carmelites came to Ireland around 1271 and established their first foundations at Leighlinbridge, County Carlow and Whitefriar Street, Dublin. By 1500 there were twenty-five friaries throughout the country. However, the Act of Dissolution of Henry VIII (1536) took a heavy toll; within a few years many friaries were either closed or destroyed. Though greatly weakened by the Reformation and by the Cromwellian persecution, at no time did the Order disappear completely from Ireland.

In those difficult times the remaining friars continued the Carmelite charism or tradition of being in the midst of the people, often underground, but serving through word and sacrament.

From about 1720 there were foundations in Ashe Street and French Street in Dublin. In the Provincial Chapter of 1741 priors were named for fourteen of the ancient friaries including Dublin, Ballinasmale, Knocktopher, Castlelyons, Leighlinbridge, Kinsale and Ardnacranny (near Moate).

Catholic Emancipation was granted in 1829 and the Carmelites soon responded to the need for Catholic education by establishing schools wherever they had friaries. Though their numbers were still small, the Irish Province began to make a contribution to the spread of the Order by sending friars to Australia (1881) and New York (1889). In the 1920s the Irish Carmelites began the reestablishment of the Order in Britain. These three are now autonomous provinces. In 1949 the medieval friary at Aylesford was reacquired by the Order.

A major undertaking of the Irish Province was the establishment in 1946 of a mission in Southern Rhodesia, now Zimbabwe, where there is today a strong and active local presence with a Zimbabwean born regional superior.

In Ireland Carmelites have the care of three parishes in Dublin: Whitefriar Street – also an important and historic city centre church – Knocklyon and Beaumont. In County Kilkenny the parish of Ballyhale is served from the friary at Knocktopher. People come to these, and to the other Carmelite churches at Kinsale, Kildare, Moate, Knocktopher, Terenure College and Gort Muire, for Mass and other services.

Irish Carmelites are still committed to education at various levels; Terenure College, Whitefriar Street, the Milltown Institute and Zimbabwe are all places where Carmelites are engaged in this ministry.

Thus the Carmelite charism of being a contemplative fraternity in the midst of the people has had many expressions throughout more than 700 years. At present Carmelites are involved in a variety of ministries including pastoral care, spirituality, ministry to the sick, chaplaincies, retreats and lectures, and publication in the media of print and internet.

The Order is still evolving and the Irish Province is facing new situations in Church and society through its nine communities in Ireland and the communities in the Zimbabwean dioceses of Harare and Mutare. Worldwide the Carmelite Order is present in forty countries spread over all five continents.

The Discalced Carmelites, stemming from St Teresa of Avila and St John of the Cross, have four communities in Dublin and one in Loughrea and Derry respectively. The Discalced Nuns have eleven monasteries in Ireland.

The Carmelite Sisters for the Aged and Infirm have one foundation in Dalkey, Co Dublin.

CARMELITE CALENDAR

January

3 Blessed Kuriakos Elias Chavara, *priest*, d. 1871

8 St Peter Thomas, *bishop*, d. 1366

9 St Andrew Corsini, *bishop*, d. 1374

29 Blessed Archangela Giralani, *virgin*, d. 1495

March

19 St Joseph, spouse of Mary, and *principal protector of the Order*

April

1 Blessed Nuno Alvares Pereira, *religious*, d. 1431

17 Blessed Baptist Spagnoli of Mantua, *priest*, d. 1516

May

5 St Angelus, *priest and martyr*, d. c. 1240

6 Blessed Aloysius Rabatà, *priest*, d. 1490

9 St Georg Preca, *priest*, d. 1962

16 St Simon Stock, *religious*, d. c. 1265

22 St Joachina de Vedruna de Mas, *religious*, d. 1854

25 St Mary Magdalen de'Pazzi, *virgin*, d. 1607

June

14 St Elisha, *prophet*

July

9 Blessed Jane Scopelli, *virgin*, d. 1491

13 St Teresa of Jesus of 'Los Andes', *virgin*, d. 1920

16 Solemn Commemoration of the Blessed Virgin Mary of Mount Carmel

17 Blessed Teresa of St Augustine and Companions, *virgins and martyrs*, d. 1794

20 St Elijah, *Prophet and Father of Carmel*

24 Blessed John Soreth, *priest*, d. 1471

26 Sts Joachim and Anne, parents of the Virgin Mary, and *protectors of the Order.*

27 Blessed Titus Brandsma, *priest and martyr*, d. 1942

August

7 St Albert of Trapani, *priest*, d. 1307

9 St. Teresa Benedicta of the Cross (Edith Stein), *virgin and martyr*, d. 1942

17 Blessed Angelus Augustine Mazzinghi, *priest*, d. 1438

25 Blessed Mary of Jesus Crucified, *virgin*, d. 1878

September

1 St Teresa Margaret Redi, *virgin*, d. 1770

17 St Albert of Jerusalem, *bishop and lawgiver of Carmel*, d. 1214

October

1 St Thérèse of the Child Jesus, *virgin and doctor*, d. 1897

15 St Teresa of Jesus, *virgin and doctor*, d. 1582

November

5 Blessed Frances d'Amboise, *religious*, d. 1485

8 Blessed Elizabeth of the Trinity, *virgin*, d. 1906

14 All Carmelite Saints

15 Commemoration of all Carmelite Souls

19 St Raphael Kalinowski, *priest*, d. 1907

29 Blessed Denis and Redemptus, *martyrs*, d. 1638

December

5 Blessed Bartholomew Fanti, *priest*, d. 1495

14 St John of the Cross, *priest and doctor*, d. 1591

CARMELITE WEB SITES

Irish Province, O. Carm
www.carmelites.ie

   Vocations Office:
   www.carmelites.ie/Vocations/vocations.htm

International Carmelite Index
www.carmelites.info

British Province of Carmelites
www.carmelite.org

Anglo-Irish Province of Discalced Carmelites
www.ocd.ie

Carmelite Institute of Britain and Ireland
(Distance learning)
www.cibi.ie

Carmelite Forum of Britain and Ireland
www.carmeliteforum.org

ACKNOWLEDGEMENTS

The publishers and the editors are grateful to the following for permission to use material which is in their copyright: Edizioni Carmelitane, Via Sforza Pallavicini 10, Roma for Carmelite Liturgical texts; Institute of Carmelite Studies, Washington DC for extracts from *The Collected Works of St John of the Cross*, (revised 1991); *The Complete Works of Elizabeth of the Trinity*, vol 1 (1984); *The Prayers of St Thérèse of Lisieux* (1997); *The Collected Works of St Teresa of Avila*, vol 3 (1985); Br Lawrence of the Resurrection, *The Practice of the Presence of God* (1994); Edith Stein, *Collected Works*, vol 4 *The Hidden Life* (1994), Copyright © Washington Province of Discalced Carmelites, Inc. ICS Publications, 2131 Lincoln Road, N.E., Washington, DC 20002, U.S.A. www.icspublications.org, http://www.icspublications.org ; Carmelite Monastery, Tallow, Co Waterford for the prayer to St Terese; Mrs J. R. Peacey for the hymn by J. R. Peacey; the Board of Directors of Trinity College Dublin for permission to use the page from the Carmelite Rule (probably 14th century) MS 194 Trinity College, Dublin; Edmund Ross Studios, Dublin for photographs on pp 6, 10, 18, 22, 26, 86, 122, 134, 139; British Province of Carmelites for the photograph of the Reliquary of St Simon Stock at

The Friars, Aylesford, Kent; the friars of the Irish Province of Carmelites for their co-operation. Where unattributed, prayers are either composed by the editors or are believed to be traditional.